"This series is a tremendous resource for those w[a]... understanding of how the gospel is woven throu[gh]... ...gospel-minded pastors and scholars doing gospel business from all the Scriptures. This is a biblical and theological feast preparing God's people to apply the entire Bible to all of life with heart and mind wholly committed to Christ's priorities."

> **BRYAN CHAPELL,** President Emeritus, Covenant Theological Seminary; Senior Pastor, Grace Presbyterian Church, Peoria, Illinois

"Mark Twain may have smiled when he wrote to a friend, 'I didn't have time to write you a short letter, so I wrote you a long letter.' But the truth of Twain's remark remains serious and universal, because well-reasoned, compact writing requires extra time and extra hard work. And this is what we have in the Crossway Bible study series *Knowing the Bible*. The skilled authors and notable editors provide the contours of each book of the Bible as well as the grand theological themes that bind them together as one Book. Here, in a 12-week format, are carefully wrought studies that will ignite the mind and the heart."

> **R. KENT HUGHES,** Visiting Professor of Practical Theology, Westminster Theological Seminary

"*Knowing the Bible* brings together a gifted team of Bible teachers to produce a high-quality series of study guides. The coordinated focus of these materials is unique: biblical content, provocative questions, systematic theology, practical application, and the gospel story of God's grace presented all the way through Scripture."

> **PHILIP G. RYKEN,** President, Wheaton College

"These *Knowing the Bible* volumes provide a significant and very welcome variation on the general run of inductive Bible studies. This series provides substantial instruction, as well as teaching through the very questions that are asked. *Knowing the Bible* then goes even further by showing how any given text links with the gospel, the whole Bible, and the formation of theology. I heartily endorse this orientation of individual books to the whole Bible and the gospel, and I applaud the demonstration that sound theology was not something invented later by Christians, but is right there in the pages of Scripture."

> **GRAEME L. GOLDSWORTHY,** former lecturer, Moore Theological College; author, *According to Plan, Gospel and Kingdom, The Gospel in Revelation,* and *Gospel and Wisdom*

"What a gift to earnest, Bible-loving, Bible-searching believers! The organization and structure of the Bible study format presented through the *Knowing the Bible* series is so well conceived. Students of the Word are led to understand the content of passages through perceptive, guided questions, and they are given rich insights and application all along the way in the brief but illuminating sections that conclude each study. What potential growth in depth and breadth of understanding these studies offer! One can only pray that vast numbers of believers will discover more of God and the beauty of his Word through these rich studies."

> **BRUCE A. WARE,** Professor of Christian Theology, The Southern Baptist Theological Seminary

K N O W I N G   T H E   B I B L E

J. I. Packer, Theological Editor
Dane C. Ortlund, Series Editor
Lane T. Dennis, Executive Editor

•   •   •   •   •   •

Genesis	Ecclesiastes	John	Colossians/
Exodus	Isaiah	Acts	Philemon
Leviticus	Jeremiah	Romans	Hebrews
Joshua	Daniel	1 Corinthians	James
Ruth, Esther	Hosea	2 Corinthians	Revelation
Ezra, Nehemiah	Matthew	Galatians	
Psalms	Mark	Ephesians	
Proverbs	Luke	Philippians	

•   •   •   •   •   •

J. I. PACKER is Board of Governors' Professor of Theology at Regent College (Vancouver, BC). Dr. Packer earned his DPhil at the University of Oxford. He is known and loved worldwide as the author of the best-selling book *Knowing God*, as well as many other titles on theology and the Christian life. He serves as the General Editor of the ESV Bible and as the Theological Editor for the *ESV Study Bible*.

LANE T. DENNIS is President of Crossway, a not-for-profit publishing ministry. Dr. Dennis earned his PhD from Northwestern University. He is Chair of the ESV Bible Translation Oversight Committee and Executive Editor of the *ESV Study Bible*.

DANE C. ORTLUND is Executive Vice President of Bible Publishing and Bible Publisher at Crossway. He is a graduate of Covenant Theological Seminary (MDiv, ThM) and Wheaton College (BA, PhD). Dr. Ortlund has authored several books and scholarly articles in the areas of Bible, theology, and Christian living.

LEVITICUS

A 12-WEEK STUDY

Michael LeFebvre

:: CROSSWAY®

WHEATON, ILLINOIS

Crossway is a publishing ministry of Good News Publishers.

VP		26	25	24	23	22	21	20	19	18	17	16
15	14	13	12	11	10	9	8	7	6	5	4	3	2	1

TABLE OF CONTENTS

KNOWING THE BIBLE, as the series title indicates, was created to help readers know and understand the meaning, the message, and the God of the Bible. Each volume in the series consists of 12 units that progressively take the reader through a clear, concise study of that book of the Bible. In this way, any given volume can fruitfully be used in a 12-week format either in group study, such as in a church-based context, or in individual study. Of course, these 12 studies could be completed in fewer or more than 12 weeks, as convenient, depending on the context in which they are used.

Each study unit gives an overview of the text at hand before digging into it with a series of questions for reflection or discussion. The unit then concludes by highlighting the gospel of grace in each passage ("Gospel Glimpses"), identifying whole-Bible themes that occur in the passage ("Whole-Bible Connections"), and pinpointing Christian doctrines that are affirmed in the passage ("Theological Soundings").

The final component to each unit is a section for reflecting on personal and practical implications from the passage at hand. The layout provides space for recording responses to the questions proposed, and we think readers need to do this to get the full benefit of the exercise. The series also includes definitions of key words. These definitions are indicated by a note number in the text and are found at the end of each chapter.

Lastly, for help in understanding the Bible in this deeper way, we would urge the reader to use the ESV Bible and the *ESV Study Bible,* which are available online at www.esvbible.org. The *Knowing the Bible* series is also available online. Additional 12-week studies covering each book of the Bible will be added as they become available.

May the Lord greatly bless your study as you seek to know him through knowing his Word.

J. I. Packer
Lane T. Dennis

WEEK 1: OVERVIEW

Getting Acquainted

Leviticus—the center book of the Pentateuch (the first five books of the Bible)—reveals the heart of Old Testament law.[1] Portions of the law teach the holiness God requires of his people. Other portions teach the forgiveness God offers to restore sinners to holiness. The major focus of Leviticus is atonement,[2] God's provision for forgiveness. Readers often find Leviticus difficult to understand since it is written in the language of ancient ritual, with rules about festivals, sacrifices, ritual washings, and the like. Nevertheless, rich lessons on the atonement offered through Christ will reward those who undertake its study.

As we begin our study of Leviticus, it will help to bear in mind that ritual is "acted theology." Rituals are prescribed actions whereby the Old Testament people of God expressed and passed on what they believed about sin[3] and atonement. Their method of expressing faith (i.e., ritual) is unfamiliar to many modern readers; but as we explore the Levitical rites in this study, the truths confessed by Old Testament believers will become delightfully familiar to New Testament Christians.

Reading Leviticus is like rummaging through an old chest in the attic. Though confronted with many strange items from a bygone era, the photos you encounter present faces of ancestors with a striking resemblance to your own. Likewise, the rituals of Leviticus are unfamiliar relics of a bygone era, but in them we discern the early outlines of the same gospel[4] we cherish as Christians. (For further background, see the *ESV Study Bible*, pages 211–216; available online at www.esvbible.org.)

7

Placing It in the Larger Story

Leviticus is the third of the five Books of Moses (Genesis, Exodus, Leviticus, Numbers, and Deuteronomy). Exodus brought the people out of Egypt to Mount Sinai, where the tabernacle was constructed. Numbers will take the people from Mount Sinai to the border of the Promised Land. Nestled in between those two books, Leviticus takes place during the course of one month at the foot of Mount Sinai (Ex. 40:17; Num. 1:1). It was the first month of the tabernacle's operation, when the people learned lessons on communion with God, who dwelt in their midst. The book's rich descriptions of sacrifices, moral holiness, and ritual purity provided ancient Israel with a gripping vision for living at one ("at-one-ment") with God.

The New Testament teaches that Jesus came to fulfill the atonement taught in the Old Testament law (Matt. 5:17). That means the rituals of the law should no longer be practiced (Heb. 8:13; 10:1), but it also means that we can gain insight into Christ's work by studying those rituals (Luke 24:27). The Old Testament law (including Leviticus) is like the blueprints of a building: once the building is finished, its blueprints are no longer needed, but they are still useful for understanding the finished product. When we study these "blueprints" of atonement, we explore the riches of what Christ came to fulfill.

Key Verse

"The life of the flesh is in the blood, and I have given it for you on the altar to make atonement for your souls, for it is the blood that makes atonement by the life" (Lev. 17:11).

Date and Historical Background

It is not clear how soon Leviticus was written after the events it records. Scholars have advanced numerous theories concerning the production of the Pentateuch (including Leviticus), but there is no conclusive reason to question the testimony preserved within Scripture. Moses is identified in Leviticus itself as the one who received the laws from God contained in its pages, and Moses is elsewhere described as writing down various collections of the laws God gave at Mount Sinai (Ex. 24:4, 7; Deut. 31:9, 24). For these reasons, Moses has traditionally been recognized as the primary author of the entire Pentateuch, including Leviticus. That would mean Leviticus was originally written during Moses' lifetime, in the fifteenth or thirteenth century BC.

Outline

The outline used in this study is based on the presence of a pattern called *chiasm*. In a chiasm, the first half of the text presents a series of topics, which the second half repeats in reverse order. The center of the chiasm (where the two halves meet) is the focal point of the text. The following chiasm points to the Day of Atonement (IV) as the focus of Leviticus. Three topic categories are repeated in mirror image on both sides of that center: Sacrifices (I/VII), Priesthood (II/VI), and Cleanness/Holiness (III/V). The closing set of Blessings and Curses (VIII) is located outside the chiasm as a seal to close the book.

I. Sacrifices (1:1–7:38)

II. Priesthood: Its Appointment (8:1–10:20)

III. Laws of Clean and Unclean (11:1–15:33)

IV. Day of Atonement (16:1–34)

V. Laws of Holy and Unholy (17:1–20:27)

VI. Priesthood: Its Continuation (21:1–22:33)

VII. Sacrifice Festivals (23:1–25:55)

VIII. Blessings, Discipline, and Responses (26:1–27:34)

As You Get Started

Have you ever studied or heard a sermon series about Leviticus? What key lessons have you learned from Leviticus in the past, and what do you hope to gain from this study?

Have you ever studied the New Testament book of Hebrews, which offers significant interpretations for several important rituals from Leviticus? What have you learned about the Old Testament festivals and sacrifices from Hebrews or other New Testament books?

A wedding ceremony is one setting in which rituals are still commonly practiced. As we think about how rituals express beliefs, discuss several symbolic
aspects of a wedding and the truths about marriage expressed by those actions.

Jesus came to be the "Lamb of God, who takes away the sin of the world" (John
1:29). How do you expect this study of Leviticus to help you grow in grace and
joy in Christ?

As You Finish This Unit . . .

**Read Hebrews 9:23–28 and pray for God's Spirit to enrich your faith in Christ
through your study of Leviticus's shadows of his work of atonement.**

Definitions

[1] **Law** – When spelled with an initial capital letter, "Law" refers to the first five books of the Bible (see also Pentateuch). The law contains numerous commands of God to his people, including the Ten Commandments and instructions regarding worship, sacrifice, and life in Israel. The NT often uses "the law" (lower case) to refer to the entire body of precepts set forth in the books of the Law.

[2] **Atonement** – The reconciliation of a person with God, often associated with the offering of a sacrifice. Through his death and resurrection, Jesus Christ made atonement for the sins of believers. His death satisfied God's just wrath against sinful humanity, just as OT sacrifices symbolized substitutionary death as payment for sin.

[3] **Sin** – Any violation of or failure to adhere to the commands of God, or the desire to do so.

[4] **Gospel** – A common translation for a Greek word meaning "good news," that is, the good news of Jesus Christ and the salvation he made possible by his crucifixion, burial, and resurrection. "Gospel" with an initial capital letter refers to each of the biblical accounts of Jesus' life on earth (Matthew, Mark, Luke, and John).

WEEK 2: OFFERING THE SACRIFICES

Leviticus 1:1–6:7

▲

The Place of the Passage

Leviticus begins with sacrifice instructions. There were five kinds of sacrifices used in Old Testament worship: burnt offerings (1:1–17), grain offerings (2:1–16), peace offerings (3:1–17), sin offerings (4:1–5:13), and guilt offerings (5:14–6:7). These offerings were all part of a process called "making atonement" (note the repetition of that phrase throughout this passage). The process of atonement is too rich for just one kind of sacrifice to represent it, so Leviticus appoints five sacrifice rituals to express different aspects of the singular work of atonement.

The Big Picture

The people of Israel are able to enter God's presence because of the thorough system of atonement he put in place.

> ### Reflection and Discussion

Read each of the five sacrifice sections one at a time, using the provided questions to guide your reflection after each reading.

Burnt Offerings (1:1–17)

For this offering, the entire sacrifice was burned as a "food offering with a pleasing aroma to the LORD" (vv. 9, 13, 17). God does not literally consume food (Ps. 50:13), but this sacrifice uses a common human experience to portray God's pleasure. How does the "pleasing aroma" of cooking food help you identify with the pleasure of God in this sacrifice?

The burnt offering instructions are repeated three times, for those who bring cattle (Lev. 1:3–9), sheep or goats (vv. 10–13), and birds (vv. 14–17). What does this sequence indicate about the economic conditions in Hebrew society and equal access for all to the atonement?

Grain Offerings (2:1–16)

This is the only offering that does not involve blood, hence its traditional title "grain offering." Its Hebrew title, however, is *minhah*, which means "tribute." What do you think it means to bring a tribute offering (*minhah*) to the heavenly King upon entering his house? (Compare 1 Sam. 10:27, where the men of Israel refused to bring such a "present" [*minhah*] to King Saul.)

Peace Offerings (3:1–17)

The burnt offering was wholly burned on the altar. The grain offering was partially burned and partially eaten by priests. The peace offering is the only sacrifice from which the offerer himself ate a portion. This was done in the presence of God, who also received a portion on the altar (see 7:11–36). What is the significance of calling this a peace[1] offering? (Compare Gen. 31:44–46.)

The previous three offerings were marked by the repeated phrase, "It shall be a food offering to the LORD." The final two sacrifice categories feature the repeated phrase, "He shall be forgiven" (Lev. 4:26, 31, 35; 5:10, 13, 16, 18; 6:7). All five sacrifices are about sin and its forgiveness,[2] but the first three use meal imagery to emphasize communion with God restored by sacrifice, while the last two emphasize sin's removal through sacrifice.

Sin Offerings (4:1–5:13)

The sin offering treats sacrificial blood like a detergent that washes the "stains" of human sin from God's presence. It is the offensiveness of sin against God— and its removal—that this offering teaches. Look at the following verses and note how different categories of sin penetrate more deeply into God's house. What do you think about different sins causing different degrees of offense against God: a priest's sin or congregation-wide sin (4:5–7, 16–18); a ruler's or an individual's sin (4:25, 30)?

Old Testament law distinguished "unintentional" sins from "high-handed" (or deliberate) sins (see Num. 15:22–31). The sin offering removed the offense of unintentional sins (4:2, 13, 22, 27; cf., 5:14, 18). High-handed sins could also be cleansed, but only by the intercession of the high priest on the Day of Atonement (Lev. 16:16, 21). What does the distinction between unintentional and high-handed sin suggest about God's perspective on sin? Many think that sins incur guilt only when committed intentionally; what does it imply about the true human condition that so much provision was made even for "unintentional" sins?

Guilt Offerings (5:14–6:7)

This class of offering was to repair the economic damage that sins often cause. Sin can bring loss to God's house (5:14–19) or to a neighbor (6:1–7). In Old Testament law, a person who concealed theft and was caught had to pay double or even fivefold restitution (Ex. 22:1, 4). But in this text we learn that one who confessed his sin voluntarily, restored the loss, and brought a guilt offering paid only an added fifth in penalty (Lev. 6:5). Notably, one-fifth (or 20 percent) was a typical interest rate on loans in the ancient world. What does this indicate about God's attitude toward those who repent[3] voluntarily versus those who must be confronted about their sins?

Read through the following three sections on *Gospel Glimpses, Whole-Bible Connections,* and *Theological Soundings.* Then take time to consider the *Personal Implications* these sections may have for you.

Gospel Glimpses

ACCEPTED. The opening verses of Leviticus introduce its gospel orientation: "When any one of you brings an offering to the LORD [lit., draws near to the LORD with an offering], . . . he shall bring it to the entrance of the tent of meeting, *that he may be accepted before the LORD*" (Lev. 1:2–3). What a marvelous privilege it is to be invited to draw near to God and to approach him with the promise of acceptance!

LAMB OF GOD. Early in Israel's history, God taught Abraham about *the* sacrifice that would ultimately atone for sin. God took Abraham to the mountain where the temple would later be built (Gen. 22:2; 2 Chron. 3:1). There he was told to sacrifice his beloved son Isaac, the heir of the promised kingdom. However, before Abraham could carry through with that daunting command, God gave a ram as a substitute for Isaac. By that exchange, God taught that every animal offered at his sanctuary foreshadowed an heir greater than Isaac who would one day become the true sacrifice. Thus the author of Genesis closes that story with the statement, "So ... it is said to this day, 'On the mount of the LORD it [or "he"] shall be provided'" (Gen. 22:14). When the book of Genesis was composed, the people of God were still looking forward to the promised heir who would fulfill the sacrifice represented by all the animal offerings on the sanctuary altar. The Psalms and the Prophets also express this hope in the Coming One's sacrifice: see especially Psalm 16:8–11 (compare Acts 2:25–28); Psalm 22:1–31 (compare Matt. 27:46); Psalm 40:6–8 (compare Heb. 10:5–10); and Isaiah 53:1–12 (compare Acts 8:32–35). Although some in ancient Israel trusted the animal sacrifices themselves as the literal payment for their forgiveness (Ps. 50:7–15; Isa. 1:11), the true purpose of the sacrifices was always to point ahead to the sacrifice of Christ.

Whole-Bible Connections

COMMUNION. The peace offering involved five steps: presentation of a spotless offering (Lev. 3:1, 6); laying hands on the sacrifice (3:2, 7–8, 13); slaughter (3:2, 8, 13); offering a portion to God (3:3–5, 9–11, 14–16); and eating a portion in God's house (7:11–36). In the New Testament, Jesus sat with his disciples at a peace offering meal (Luke 22:7–23) and revealed that he is the true sacrifice who provides for our communion at the Lord's Table. Therefore, Jesus instructed his disciples to eat a simplified peace offering meal "in remembrance of me." Now, instead of bringing an animal sacrifice, Christians approach the communion table by remembering Christ with repentance in his name (1 Cor. 11:17–34).

Theological Soundings

SUBSTITUTIONARY ATONEMENT. Each time an animal sacrifice was brought to the altar, the offerer would "lay his hand on [its] head ... and it [was] accepted for him" (Lev. 1:4; also, 3:2, 8, 13; 4:4, 15, 24, 29, 33). The ritual act of pressing one's hand on the head of the offering was an act of transfer, identifying the animal as a substitute to take the presenter's place in the ritual to follow. This action was often accompanied with a verbal confession of sins over the animal (16:21). These Old Testament ritual acts provide the backdrop for the reality that the sinless Christ became a substitute for sinners.

Personal Implications

Take time to reflect on the lessons on atonement symbolized in the offerings in Leviticus 1:1–6:7 as they minister to your own faith today. Make notes below on personal implications of the (1) *Gospel Glimpses*, (2) *Whole-Bible Connections*, (3) *Theological Soundings*, and (4) this passage as a whole.

1. Gospel Glimpses

2. Whole-Bible Connections

3. Theological Soundings

4. Leviticus 1:1–6:7

As You Finish This Unit . . .

Praise God that he loved the Old Testament saints so much to give them such vivid lessons about the coming Messiah and his sacrifice. Thank God that he has faithfully fulfilled those ceremonies by providing his people with Jesus, the true Lamb of God. Examine your own heart to confess your sin and trust the sacrifice of Christ as your own basis for forgiveness and acceptance by God.

Definitions

[1] **Peace** – In modern use, the absence of tension or conflict. In biblical use, a condition of well-being or wholeness that God grants his people, which also results in harmony with God and others.

[2] **Forgiveness** – Release from guilt and the reestablishment of relationship. Forgiveness can be granted by God to human beings (Luke 24:47; 1 John 1:9) and by human beings to those who have wronged them (Matt. 18:21–22; Col. 3:13).

[3] **Repentance** – A complete change of heart and mind regarding one's overall attitude toward God or one's individual actions. True regeneration and conversion is always accompanied by repentance.

WEEK 3: SHARING THE SACRIFICE MEALS

Leviticus 6:8–7:38

The Place of the Passage

The ultimate goal for the forgiveness of sins is to restore communion with God. Leviticus emphasizes this lesson by including with the rules about sacrifices a separate section describing the ritual meal accompanying each sacrifice. In the modern West, mealtime rarely has the same significance it did in biblical times. It is easy, therefore, to overlook the importance of this ritual meal in God's house as the culmination of the sacrifice. Having already discussed the sacrifice procedures for all five categories of offerings (1:1–6:7), Leviticus revisits all five offerings again, this time with particular focus on how the resulting fellowship meals were to be eaten in the Lord's house (6:8–7:38).

The Big Picture

The goal of atonement is fellowship between God (the host), the priest[1] (who accomplishes our atonement), and the people (whose sins are purged by the atonement).

> ## Reflection and Discussion

Instruction for eating the various sacrifices is given in three groups: the one offering wholly consumed by God (6:8–13); the three offerings consumed by God and the priests (6:14–7:10); and the one offering meal shared by God, the priests, and the people (7:11–38). Read these three sections one at a time as outlined below, pausing to respond to the reflection questions after each reading.

Consuming the Burnt Offering (6:8–13)

The burnt offering was consumed wholly on the altar. It was kept burning around the clock, replaced daily (compare Ex. 29:38–42). The other sacrifices were piled on top of this one and carried heavenward in its flames (6:12). How would an ancient Hebrew believer have felt, knowing that wherever he or she was at any time of the day, a "pleasing aroma" was rising to God for his or her atonement?

Consuming the Grain, Sin, and Guilt Offerings (6:14–7:10)

These three offerings are shared between the altar and the attending priests. Using the following chart (which is an outline of this passage), note the locations where the various portions are to be consumed.

	Grain Offering	Sin Offering	Guilt Offering
The Lord's Portion	6:14–15	6:24–25	7:1–5
The Priests' Portion	6:16–18	6:26–29	7:6–7
Exceptions to the Norm	6:19–23	6:30	

20

When offerings are presented at the temple, the entire offering becomes the Lord's. It is the Lord who gives portions of the sacrifice food back to the priests (6:17), thereby honoring their work in accomplishing the people's atonement (7:7). How does this expression of God's pleasure in the work of the priests serve as a backdrop to New Testament passages like John 10:17–18?

Consuming the Peace Offering (7:11–38)

The final sacrifice meal is the one consumed by God (on the altar), the priest, and the offerer together. Its instructions begin with four warnings (vv. 11–27). The last of these—prohibiting consumption of the sacrifice's blood (vv. 26–27)—is especially significant. Some ancient religions required worshipers to consume blood in order to unite the offerer's life with that of the offering ("the life of every creature is its blood"; 17:14). What do you think it means that Old Testament believers were not to partake of the animal's blood (being a foreshadowing of the true sacrifice), yet the New Testament communion table (the fulfillment of the peace offering meal) includes ritual participation in Christ's blood (Mark 14:23–24)?

Leviticus 7:28–36 gives instructions for dividing the peace offering meal into portions. Once again the text emphasizes this is the "Lord's food offering." He is the one who takes a portion for himself (v. 31) and grants portions of it to the mediating priests (vv. 32–36) and the offerer (vv. 11–30). How should the depiction of God as the host in this Old Testament peace meal inform the

Christian's attitude toward the communion table (Luke 22:14–23) and the coming feast in heaven (Rev. 19:6–9)?

Read through the following three sections on *Gospel Glimpses, Whole-Bible Connections,* and *Theological Soundings*. Then take time to consider the *Personal Implications* these sections may have for you.

Gospel Glimpses

HEAVENLY HOST. Mealtime does not have the same significance in the modern West as in many other cultures. A meal in America is typically a pragmatic affair, sometimes as shallow as wolfing down a burger and fries in a room crowded with a dozen complete strangers. Mealtime had much greater significance in an ancient Near Eastern society like Israel. To host people in your home, feeding them at your table, was a gesture of honor. The Old Testament temple was set up not simply as an auditorium to listen to sermons and to sing but as a divine palace where the heavenly King hosted his people for feasting. Visits to the temple for sacrifice festivals were only occasional, but they represented the hope of one day dwelling forever in the presence of God (Ps. 23:6; Heb. 4:8–9; 10:1, 19–25; 12:22–24).

MEDIATOR. The Old Testament priests were imperfect individuals, requiring sacrifices for their own forgiveness before they could present sacrifices for the people (Heb. 5:1–4). Nevertheless, their presence taught that it was impossible for the people to accomplish atonement for themselves; a priestly office, wholly devoted to intercession on behalf of the people, was necessary. The ideal described in these rituals was fulfilled when the sinless Mediator appeared who was able to serve as both our High Priest and our Sacrifice (Heb. 5:5–10).

Whole-Bible Connections

HOSPITALITY. There is hardly a page of the Bible without food on it. From the garden of Eden (Gen. 2:9) to the wedding feast of the Lamb (Rev. 19:9), the

Scriptures are filled with markers of God's hospitality to us and the calling for God's people to show hospitality to others. The provision of the atonement meal in God's house is the theological anchor for all gestures of hospitality in every other corner of the Bible and in church life.

Theological Soundings

SACRAMENT. Scholars who study ancient religions observe two kinds of rituals in different cultures. One is "instrumental" (or magical) rites. Ancient rituals of this type were believed to produce an actual effect in the divine realm by prescribed manipulation of ritual objects in the human realm. Like flipping a light switch within reach to turn on a light beyond reach, magical rites sought to manipulate divine power from below. The other category of rituals is "analogical" (or sacramental) rites. This type of ritual is performed in order to identify with and respond to divine realities. The Old Testament prohibition of eating blood (thus barring literal, magical identification with animal sacrifices) is one of numerous indications that the rituals of Old Testament religion were sacramental and not magical by design. Old Testament rituals were not to be used to manipulate divine results (as magic) but rather as worship ceremonies on earth that lay claim upon heavenly realities (Ex. 25:40; Heb. 8:5; 12:18–24). One of the common errors of both Old Testament (Isa. 1:11–20; Jer. 7:8–15; Amos 5:8–27) and New Testament (Gal. 2:15–21; 3:1–9) worshipers has been the misuse of worship as a way to win heaven's blessings (instrumental rites) rather than as means to identify by faith in blessings already secured for us in heaven (sacramental rites).

Personal Implications

Take time to reflect on lessons you have learned about communion with God through the sacrifice meal instructions in Leviticus 6:8–7:38. Make notes below on personal implications of the (1) *Gospel Glimpses*, (2) *Whole-Bible Connections*, (3) *Theological Soundings*, and (4) this passage as a whole.

1. Gospel Glimpses

2. Whole-Bible Connections

3. Theological Soundings

4. Leviticus 6:8–7:38

As You Finish This Unit . . .

The next time you participate in communion, imagine you are partaking at a table that extends all the way back to the Old Testament believers, eating in the courts of the temple, and all the way forward to the saints gathered to feast in heaven itself, with Jesus and the apostles eating together in the upper room in the shadow of the cross at the center of the table. Praise God for the joy of so great a salvation that removes our sin and secures such a profound fellowship with all God's people in his house!

Definition

[1] **Priest** – In OT Israel, the priest represented the people before God, and God before the people. Only those descended from Aaron could be priests. Their prescribed duties also included inspecting and receiving sacrifices from the people and overseeing the daily activities and maintenance of the tabernacle or temple.

WEEK 4: INTRODUCING THE PRIESTHOOD

Leviticus 8:1–10:20

The Place of the Passage

In the previous sections, Leviticus described the sacrifices of Old Testament worship. In the next section, we are introduced to the Old Testament priesthood. Without suitable priests to perform its rituals, the tabernacle[1] would be like a machine with gears and pistons but no motion. The priests must keep the tabernacle operating. The next section of Leviticus describes the ordination[2] of the first priests (8:1–36), the first worship service led by the priests (9:1–24), and the tragic results when priests added unauthorized rituals to Israel's worship (10:1–20). As there was only one atonement, yet it took five different sacrifices to express the richness of that atonement, so there is only one high priest, yet it will take several priests and many Levites (though the Levites are not ordained until Num. 8:5–26) to capture the full duties of the single high priest.

The Big Picture

God's gift of atonement must be accomplished for us by a faithful priest.

> ### Reflection and Discussion

Reading the details of the priests' inauguration might seem about as exciting as poring over the user manual for a new appliance. But if the appliance is a medical device whose right use may save your life, you might appreciate knowing how it works! Read the passages introducing the temple priesthood in the three portions indicated below. Stop to respond to the discussion questions provided after each reading.

Ordination of the First Priests (8:1–36)

In a ceremony similar to crowning a new monarch, Aaron's installation started with his investiture. With the congregation watching, Moses clothed Aaron with the symbols of his office (vv. 5–12), followed by the investiture of his sons (v. 13). List the items of Aaron's apparel and discuss any thoughts you have about their significance. (See also Ex. 28:1–43; 39:1–43; see also the illustration in the *ESV Study Bible*, page 208.)

Moses sprinkled anointing oil on Aaron and on the tabernacle furnishings at the same time (Lev. 8:10–12). He also applied blood to the altar (vv. 14–15) and to the right earlobes, thumbs, and big toes of Aaron and his sons at the same time (vv. 22–24). Throughout the ordination ceremony, the new priests ate and slept inside the tabernacle courts (vv. 31–35). What was the significance of such a close connection between the priests and the objects of the tabernacle, which was itself a shadow of heaven (Ex. 25:9; Heb. 8:1–6)?

First Worship Service (9:1–24)

The seven-day installation ceremony was followed by a public worship service on the eighth day. This was the first worship service under Aaron's leadership. What was the stated purpose of that worship assembly and the name given to the tent where it took place (vv. 4–6)? What can we learn about the nature of worship from this passage?

Once the rituals of atonement were completed by the priests, the service reached its climax: Aaron pronounced the benediction (vv. 22–23; compare Num. 6:22–27). Why do you suppose God added the visible mark of fire from heaven to the close of that inaugural service (Lev. 9:24)?

How many times do you find the phrase "as the LORD commanded" attached to the activities of the ordination and first worship service (chs. 8–9)? _____ (This frequent repetition is preparing for a contrast about to emerge in the next chapter.)

Nadab and Abihu's Sin (10:1–20)

Nadab and Abihu were put to death for a seemingly minor change to the prescribed instructions for their office. Some ancient Near Eastern religions used incense and fire offerings as part of their ordination ceremonies. It is possible that Nadab and Abihu borrowed an idea they had observed elsewhere to "enhance" tabernacle worship. What does the tragic end of these priests tell us about our need for an utterly faithful intercessor?

Scholars disagree whether the fire of God's wrath in 10:2 is the same fire that displayed his glory in 9:24. What do you think?

_____

_____

_____

_____

_____

_____

The closing scene (10:12–20) was truly amazing: Aaron corrected Moses on a point of ritual protocol, and Moses admitted that Aaron was right! What does Aaron's precise ritual discernment (even correcting Moses!), in contrast with Nadab and Abihu's ritual missteps, teach us about the kind of high priest the people were to expect?

_____

_____

_____

_____

_____

_____

Read through the following three sections on *Gospel Glimpses*, *Whole-Bible Connections*, and *Theological Soundings*. Then take time to consider the *Personal Implications* these sections may have for you.

Gospel Glimpses

DRAWING NEAR. Readers are often stunned that Nadab and Abihu died for their infraction. Actually, what should amaze us is that our Great High Priest mediates a perfect atonement so that we are able to approach such a holy God without fear of the same outcome! Confronting the presence of God is a life-or-death matter, and our sins deserve the fire of his just wrath. The people of Israel got it right when they "shouted and fell on their faces" (9:24)—resulting in God's benediction (not his condemnation) and in seeing his glory (rather than falling under his judgment).

Whole-Bible Connections

AARON. The name "Aaron" occurs 347 times in the Hebrew Old Testament, indicating the importance of his ordination as Israel's high priest. For the next fifteen hundred years after Aaron's installation, the house of Aaron filled a vital role in Old Testament faith and worship. We encounter his name in the Psalms, the Old Testament history books, the Prophets, and the New Testament. The significant lessons on priesthood built around Aaron's heritage began with his ordination in the present passage.

FAITH. The Old Testament repeatedly emphasizes the importance of family lines. God made a promise to the family of Adam, the house of Noah, the household of Abraham, and so forth. In Leviticus 9, it is the house of Aaron that receives a special promise from God. Often at those points in Scripture where God makes a promise to a household, however, there is a subsequent event that clarifies the requirement of faith. Though Adam had two sons, one (Cain) was judged. Though Noah had three sons, one (Ham) experienced God's curse. Though Abraham had two sons, one (Ishmael) was sent away. And in Leviticus 8–10, the priesthood was appointed to Aaron's house, yet Nadab and Abihu were judged while faithful Eleazar and Ithamar were blessed. This frequent Old Testament lesson is interpreted in the New Testament as showing the necessity of faith for those born into the community of God's promises (Romans 9–11).

Theological Soundings

FAITHFUL WORSHIP. When societies experience revolution, the changes that take place are usually political. A new government system is put in place, or sometimes an older political system is restored. In the Bible, however, the various revolutions and reformations experienced by Israel are primarily about worship. Certainly there are political changes in Israel's history. But the Bible places special emphasis on the deformation and reformation of worship (e.g., Judg. 6:25–27; 1 Kings 16:29–34; 2 Kings 11–12; 2 Chronicles 15; 29, etc.) The cornerstone of this theme is laid with the story of Nadab and Abihu and the Lord's explanation that worship must faithfully reflect his glory (10:3; see also Ex. 20:4–6). The worship of God is not a realm for human innovation or experimentation.

BENEDICTION. The wording of the Aaronic benediction is not given until Numbers 6:24–26, but its location in the worship service is taught in Leviticus 9:22–23. It is because of the atoning sacrifice that the people receive the guarantee of blessing from God at the close of their worship in his house. In the New Testament, Jesus also lifted his hands to pronounce blessing on the disciples after his completion of the final atonement sacrifice (Luke 24:50), and the New Testament authors closed their epistles with benedictions (e.g., 1 Thess. 5:23; Eph. 6:23–24; Heb. 13:20–21). The benediction is much more than a fancy way to say "the end" at the close of a worship service. It is a declaration of God's favor because of his atonement.

Personal Implications

Take time to reflect on lessons you have learned about the kind of mediating priest God promised for his people in Leviticus 8:1–10:20. Make notes below on personal implications of the (1) *Gospel Glimpses*, (2) *Whole-Bible Connections*, (3) *Theological Soundings*, and (4) this passage as a whole.

1. Gospel Glimpses

2. Whole-Bible Connections

3. Theological Soundings

4. Leviticus 8:1–10:20

▶ As You Finish This Unit . . .

Give thanks to God for the privilege of worship mediated by the perfect high priest, Jesus Christ! Pray for faith and humility to worship God in Christ's name and in faithfulness to his Word.

Definitions

[1] **Tabernacle** – The tent where God dwelt on earth and communed with his people as Israel's divine king. Also referred to as the "tent of meeting" (Lev. 1:5). The temple in Jerusalem later replaced it.

[2] **Ordination** – Official investment of religious authority upon a person. In the Old Testament, priests were ordained. Most modern Christian denominations require some form of ordination for those in ministry.

WEEK 5: CLEAN AND UNCLEAN MEATS

Leviticus 11:1–47

Toward the end of the previous section, the Lord gave Aaron these instructions: "You are to distinguish between the holy and the common, and between the unclean and the clean, and you are to teach the people of Israel" (10:10–11). Those two categories are the focus for the next several sections of Leviticus: chapters 11–15 contain laws about distinguishing clean and unclean (purity laws); chapters 17–20 contain laws about distinguishing holy and common.

The purity laws extended Israel's "acted theology"[1] beyond worship into daily life. The rituals of worship expressed Israel's fellowship with the Lord in his house. Purity laws taught Israel to live as God's forgiven people in their own houses. The New Testament apostles set aside these purity laws because they were temporary "object lessons" superseded by the reality to which they pointed, completed in the work of Christ. Like sacrifices, purity laws are no longer applicable as Christian practice. But, like sacrifices, purity laws still offer rich insights into the work Christ came to accomplish. (For additional discussion of the categories clean, unclean, holy, and common, see "Interpretive Issues" in the ESV Study Bible, pages 211–213.)

The first set of purity laws distinguishes clean and unclean animals, with particular concern for the household diets of those living in the camp around the tabernacle.

The Big Picture

As the society of God's favor, Israel was a royal nation living like privileged nobility around God's palace.

Reflection and Discussion

Leviticus 11 presents dietary rules (vv. 1–23), followed by purification instructions for those who become unclean (vv. 24–40), a special category of unclean meats (vv. 41–43), and a summary of the chapter's main lesson (vv. 44–47). Read the entire chapter, then respond to the reflection questions below.

Leviticus orders its dietary regulations by realm: land (11:2–8), water (vv. 9–12), and air (vv. 13–23). How do these realms compare to those of creation in Genesis 1:20–25?

These rules permitted the Hebrew household a selection of meats one step below the exclusive "menu" permitted at the Lord's table (the sacrifice animals) and one step above that available to Gentiles. What is the significance of this diet assigned to the Israelites encamped between the tabernacle and the world?

The Old Testament prophets repeatedly condemn Gentile nations for their sins against God's moral laws, but Gentile nations are never condemned for not observing dietary laws. Why were these dietary laws unique to Israel?

In a farming society, removal of dead animals is part of life. Note the repeated references to one who "touches" (Lev. 11:24, 27, 31, 36, 39) dead animals or "carries their carcass" (vv. 25, 28, 40). The text does not condemn the necessary removal of, for instance, a dead hyena from one's property or a dead mouse from one's food storage. Touching something unclean is not sinful. But every contact with a carcass rendered the individual unclean overnight. What would the Old Testament believer learn by being declared ritually unclean after every contact with death?

One final category of dietary restriction is added at the end of the chapter: swarming things. From this category, nothing at all was to be eaten. Note the kind of "swarming thing" that is first on the list to be detested: "whatever goes on its belly" (v. 42). Why, as a lesson on faith, might there be a special category of rejection for swarming things, starting with "whatever goes on its belly"? (Compare Gen. 3:14–15.)

Whatever the logic behind these dietary classifications, the faith lesson is stated in the summary (Lev. 11:44–47). Compare this reason with the similar statement in Leviticus 20:24–26 and the apostle Peter's discussion of the dietary rules in Acts 10:9–29. In your own words, how were the dietary laws fulfilled at Christ's coming?

_____

_____

_____

_____

_____

_____

Read through the following three sections on *Gospel Glimpses*, *Whole-Bible Connections*, and *Theological Soundings*. Then take time to consider the *Personal Implications* these sections may have for you.

▶ Gospel Glimpses

DELIVERANCE. The summary verses at the end of this chapter (Lev. 11:44–47) state that these dietary laws were designed as a reminder that God delivered his people from bondage in Egypt to make them holy unto himself. Whatever the particular logic for marking certain animals as clean and others as unclean (see "Creation Ideal," below, for one possible explanation), every meal in Israel was to be a reminder of the congregation's special status as a people delivered from sin and bondage.

CREATION IDEAL. The logic behind the classification of clean and unclean animals is famously difficult. There is no consensus among scholars about the reasoning behind this system. However, the system may represent an ancient understanding of creation ideals based on the opening chapters of Genesis. Indicators of this include the fact that animals are classified by realms similar to those of the creation account (Gen. 1:20–25), and a special addendum is added at the end of the passage for absolute rejection of "swarming things," beginning with "whatever goes on its belly" (Lev. 11:41–43; see Gen. 3:14). Thus the animal taxonomy in Leviticus 11 may represent a dietary vision based on Edenic categories. It may also have been designed to lead Hebrew believers to identify at every meal with the vision of a restored creation society living in God's presence.

Whole-Bible Connections

WALL OF SEPARATION. One of the most significant distinctions between the Old and New Testaments is a change in the relationship of Israel and the Gentiles. In the old covenant, Israel alone had the Spirit-filled house of worship in their midst. Therefore, Hebrew society alone was rendered "clean" by the presence of the temple. The food laws were designed to demonstrate and maintain this unique status of Israel among the nations. However, when the Spirit descended on the church in the New Testament, empowering believers for witness and worship in Spirit-filled assemblies in all nations (Acts 2:1–41), the "wall of separation" and the dividing ordinances were removed (Eph. 2:11–22). Israel did not lose its status as "clean," but now Gentiles also were made clean (see Acts 10:15, 28). Centers for worship—bringing the presence of God in grace among people—were now to be established in all nations throughout the world. The removal of the food laws as a distinction of social privilege marked a dramatic advance in the work of God's grace.

Theological Soundings

CONSECRATION. The food laws are about separation from the sin-stained world and hope in God's promise of a new kingdom of holiness and perfection. Even though the ritual categories of clean and unclean meats are no longer to be observed in the church (see "Wall of Separation," above), the lessons on consecration they teach are still relevant. The apostle Peter was one of the first leaders in the New Testament church to recognize that the dietary laws were expiring (Acts 10:9–16). Nevertheless, the truth behind them continues. Thus Peter quoted from Leviticus 11 in an epistle to Gentile churches in Asia Minor: "As obedient children, do not be conformed to the passions of your former ignorance, but as he who called you is holy, you also be holy in all your conduct, since it is written, 'You shall be holy, for I am holy'" (1 Pet. 1:14–16, quoting Lev. 11:44). Although the dietary laws themselves are obsolete, their lessons on consecration to God are still relevant.

Personal Implications

Take time to reflect on lessons you have learned about the privileged identity of the redeemed as God's people in Leviticus 11:1–47. Make notes below on personal implications of the (1) *Gospel Glimpses*, (2) *Whole-Bible Connections*, (3) *Theological Soundings*, and (4) this passage as a whole.

1. Gospel Glimpses

2. Whole-Bible Connections

3. Theological Soundings

4. Leviticus 11:1–47

As You Finish This Unit . . .

Praise God for the privilege of Gentiles being grafted into the blessings of the "olive tree" (Rom. 11:17), sharing in the salvation first revealed to Israel.

Definition

[1] **Theology** – The study of God and religious beliefs.

WEEK 6: CLEAN AND UNCLEAN BODILY CONDITIONS

Leviticus 12:1–15:33

The Place of the Passage

In this passage, we finish the section of Leviticus dealing with purity laws. The section on ritual purity (11:1–15:33) is distinct from the section of Leviticus dealing with laws about holiness (17:1–20:27). Scholars disagree over the exact difference between these two categories (see *ESV Study Bible*, page 212). One possibility—and the view explored in this study guide—is that holiness laws identify sins, like sexual immorality (see Lev. 18:1–30), while purity laws identify life's brokenness due to human sinfulness. The blood loss experienced during childbirth, for example, is definitely not sinful (thus it is not "unholy"). Nevertheless, blood loss and its attendant pain are a reminder of sin's curse on an otherwise good aspect of human life. Thus it is called "unclean" (see Lev. 12:1–8; compare Gen. 3:16). Within this way of understanding Israel's purity laws as distinct from the holiness laws, the ritual requirements in this section of Leviticus would have reminded Israel that life's brokenness has no enduring place among a people dwelling in God's presence. The atonement promises not only forgiveness of sins but the reversal of its curse and its effects as well.

The Big Picture

Because God atones for sin and dwells among his people, we are to anticipate the end of sin's curse on our daily lives and a resurrection from sickness and death.

39

Reflection and Discussion

This passage is constructed as a chiasm, as shown in the following outline. This structure places emphasis on the center point (c)—the rituals of restoration for one healed of leprosy:

a. Reproduction discharges: childbirth (12:1–8)

   b. Leprosy laws for flesh and garments (13:1–59)

      c. Restoration after healing (14:1–32)

   b'. Leprosy laws for houses (14:33–55)

a'. Reproduction discharges: conception (15:1–33)

The following reading selections are grouped topically based on the above outline. Read each selection as indicated below, stopping after each reading to respond to the reflection guidance provided.

Reproductive Discharges (12:1–8; 15:1–33)

This is one of those "PG-13" portions of Scripture that make many readers uncomfortable. Why do you suppose reproductive issues were such a focal point of Levitical purity laws?

Everywhere in Scripture, bearing children is celebrated as a blessing from God. It is not sinful to have babies! Why, then, do you suppose the mother's postnatal bleeding required burnt and sin offerings to "make atonement for her" and make her clean (12:6–8)?

Consider the following outline of chapter 15. What significance do you see in this pattern and how the topic of discharges is arranged?

   a. Abnormal discharges—of a man (15:2–15)
      b. Normal discharges outside conjugal relations—of a man (15:16–17)
         c. Normal discharge in sexual intercourse—of a man with a woman (15:18)
      b'. Normal discharges outside conjugal relations—of a woman (15:19–24)
   a'. Abnormal discharges—of a woman (15:25–30)

Under what conditions would atonement sacrifices be offered (15:14–15, 29–30)? Under what circumstances were ritual washings appointed (15:6–12, 16–17, 18, 21–24, 27)?

Leviticus 15:31 states the reason for the regulations in chapter 15. Read this verse again and reflect on what you think it reveals about the significance of these purity laws as rituals of faith.

Leprosy Laws—for Persons (13:1–46)

The disease we commonly call leprosy today (Hansen's disease) is not the same condition as biblical leprosy. Furthermore, Leviticus 13 never actually defines leprosy. Instead, this chapter gives instructions on how to avoid misdiagnosing as leprosy any of seven different skin conditions (vv. 2–8, 9–17, 18–23, 24–28, 29–37, 38–39, 40–44). What does this care to avoid over-diagnosing a life-changing condition suggest about the character of these laws?

The power of death was tangibly at work in a leprous individual's flesh. For this reason, an infected person performed the rites of mourning associated with death (vv. 45–46). A common modern perception is that leprous individuals were ostracized in biblical Israel, but what do you expect the proper response by fellow Israelites would have been to such a person? (Note that those afflicted with biblical leprosy were ritually unclean, but were probably not contagious.)

Leprosy Laws—for Garments and Houses (13:47–59; 14:33–53)

The Hebrew term for leprosy (*tsara'at*) refers to the characteristic flaking of ulcerated flesh caused by the disease. The same term was used also for fungal or mold infestations in garments and buildings. This is not because they were thought to share a common cause, but because they shared similar symptoms: decay and flaking that spreads and destroys. What would be the significance of ritually highlighting leprosy and its resolution in all three layers of human covering: flesh, garment, and house?

What does it mean to "make atonement for the house" (14:53)? What does the instruction to atone, even for a house (which does not commit sin), say about the nature of atonement?

The Restoration of Persons after Leprosy (14:1–32)

Unlike Hansen's disease (often called leprosy today), biblical leprosy was not necessarily permanent. Cases of it were known to heal. This passage describes the celebration when a case of leprosy was resolved. What physical movements of location take place in the three stages of this celebration?

   a. First seven days (vv. 2–8) _____

   b. The seventh day (v. 9, moving beyond
      the restriction at the end of v. 8) _____

   c. The eighth day (vv. 10–31) _____

The disease is already healed when the ritual begins (v. 3), so these are not magical rites to remove the disease. They are rituals to testify to healing and its significance. How might the ritual with birds (vv. 4–8) fit within this acted confession of God's grace manifest in this healing?

Previously the leprous person was under the rites of death, excluded even from his own house (compare Num. 19:14). What does it signify for an individual, once marked as "dead," to be restored to his community?

Leprosy (like postnatal bleeding) was not necessarily a punishment for personal sin. (Job, whose disease may have been leprosy, was wrongly accused of bringing his disease on himself by personal sin.) Why, then, would this restoration from "living death" be sealed with sacrifices (Lev. 14:18–21, 29–31)?

Read through the following three sections on *Gospel Glimpses*, *Whole-Bible Connections*, and *Theological Soundings*. Then take time to consider the *Personal Implications* these sections may have for you.

Gospel Glimpses

RESURRECTION. This passage is one of the most vivid testimonies of Israel's faith in resurrection[1] in all of the Old Testament. Sadly, most readers get bogged down in the strangeness of its rituals and miss the beauty of the hope here captured. Each of the conditions in this passage marks the presence of death where there ought to be life. Reproductive organs were created for life. The abnormal and normal loss of life fluids in these centers of life represents the evil brought by sin. Leprosy made especially visible the presence of death and decay in the body and in the extended coverings of life—garments and homes. But each of these leprosy sections closes with rituals of restoration when the presence of death has been reversed. And the centerpiece of the collection is the extensive ritual of restoration for the person healed of leprosy. These must have been extremely joyous occasions. Such public ceremonies of restoration from "living death" ensured that all Israel knew what had taken place and that all the people should see this reversal of death as a lesson about the victory of God's atonement—resurrection. Today we no longer mark physical healing with ritual markers of resurrection, because we have the ultimate testimony of our resurrection hope to look to—the historical resurrection of Jesus.

Whole-Bible Connections

CEREMONIAL LAWS. There were many ceremonial laws observed in the Old Testament, but not as many as the growing list of rules added by the Pharisees whom Jesus confronted in the New Testament. The ceremonial laws given by

God were designed to help (even to "imprison" and compel) Old Testament believers to view all of life through the grid of God's promises and to restrain them from the temptations of surrounding nations (see Gal. 3:19). However, the onerous complexity that came to characterize the ceremonial law by New Testament times was due to the legalistic tendencies of the Pharisees, who over-interpreted the Mosaic laws and added new commandments and traditions of their own (see Matt. 15:1–9).

Theological Soundings

SIN'S CURSE. When a vandal damages someone's property, the act of vandalism (the crime) is offensive to the victim, as are its effects (the damage to the victim's property). God is the one offended by sin, in both its commission (actual sin) and its extensive impact that spreads like a cancer through all aspects of his creation (the curse of sin). Levitical holiness and purity laws taught Israel that God's provision of atonement was powerful enough both to forgive sin and to remove its stains. Purity laws in the Old Testament remind us that not only sin but also the effects of sin (our human brokenness) are offensive to the God who created us for life and wholeness. We rejoice in the ability of his atonement to reverse sin in its totality.

Personal Implications

Take time to reflect on lessons you have learned about the doctrine of resurrection in Leviticus 12:1–15:33. Make notes below on personal implications of the (1) *Gospel Glimpses*, (2) *Whole-Bible Connections*, (3) *Theological Soundings*, and (4) this passage as a whole.

1. Gospel Glimpses

2. Whole-Bible Connections

3. Theological Soundings

----

4. Leviticus 12:1–15:33

As You Finish This Unit . . .

Ancient Israel looked to rituals of resurrection attached to certain afflictions to give them hope in all their afflictions. Read the eyewitness account of the resurrection that eclipsed all those old rituals—the resurrection of Jesus—in Luke 24:1–9. Praise God for such a great resurrection hope, and exhort your own heart to view all your afflictions through the grid of resurrection faith.

Definition

[1] **Resurrection** – The impartation of new, eternal life to a dead person at the end of time (or in the case of Jesus, on the third day after his death). This new life is not a mere resuscitation of the body (as in the case of Lazarus; John 11:1–44) but a transformation of the body to an eternal state (1 Cor. 15:35–58). Both the righteous and the wicked will be resurrected, the former to eternal life and the latter to judgment (John 5:29).

WEEK 7: THE DAY OF ATONEMENT

Leviticus 16:1–34

The Place of the Passage

We have reached the centerpiece of Leviticus (see the book outline in the lesson for Week 1, above). In fact, because Leviticus is the center book of the Pentateuch,[1] this chapter could also be regarded as the heart of the entire Old Testament law. It might seem like these laws about the Day of Atonement should be included in Leviticus 23, where Israel's other festivals are found. Instead, this detailed description of the Day of Atonement is separated from the rest and placed between the purity laws (11:1–15:33) and the holiness laws (17:1–20:27) at the structural midpoint of Leviticus. Here it anchors the law to the festival day when one man—the nation's high priest—enters the throne room of God to make atonement for the whole nation.

The Big Picture

The stain and power of sin are removed when the high priest enters God's presence with the blood of our atonement.

> **Reflection and Discussion**

After introductory instructions (16:1–10), the Day of Atonement rites are presented in three stages. Read each portion below, pausing to consider the reflection questions for each section.

Preparation (16:1–10)

Atonement is too complex for a single ritual to express. In addition to the five types of sacrifice, numerous festivals contribute to the Levitical picture of atonement. What is one of the unique features of the Day of Atonement, highlighted in the opening verses (vv. 2–3) of this passage? Discuss its significance.

Several sacrifice animals are prepared for the day's events. Most peculiar are the two goats of the sin offering (v. 5). One goat would die, and the other would be "sent away into the wilderness to Azazel" (v. 10). Scholars do not know what the Hebrew word *azazel* means, which is why it is left untranslated. Here are three possibilities:

a. Azazel may be a name for the Devil, in which case this rite signified the return of sin and its consequences to fall upon the Devil's own head (compare Judg. 9:57).
b. The King James Version translates *azazel* as "scapegoat," suggesting that the word describes the goat's purpose rather than its destination.
c. The term may mean "harsh and rugged place," so that the second goat is being sent to the furthest hinterlands (the "azazel") of the wilderness (compare Lev. 14:4–7; 16:22).

Reread 16:8–10 and 20–22 and ponder which of these possible meanings of *azazel* makes the best sense to you, and why.

Atonement for the Priests (16:11–14)

Review the significance of the "sin offering" (see the Week 2 "Reflection and Discussion" notes on 4:1–5:13). What is taking place when the high priest sprinkles the blood of the "sin offering" in the holiest place?

Why must the high priest first make atonement for himself and his own house? (Compare Heb. 7:26–28.)

Atonement for the People (16:15–22)

The kinds of sins purged on the Day of Atonement are listed twice (vv. 16, 21). In each list, the term "transgressions" (Heb. *pesha*) is featured. This term refers to an act of blatant rebellion. Even high-handed sins of rebellion—the severe sins not addressed by the daily sacrifices—were atoned for on the Day of Atonement. (Review the Week 2 "Reflection and Discussion" notes on Lev. 4:1–5:13.) Why would sins of blatant rebellion (high-handed sins) require the special intercession[2] of the high priest in the tabernacle's inner sanctum?

Closing Celebrations (16:23–28)

In the final phase of the Day of Atonement, the high priest changed out of the plain, linen robe he wore for the day's sacrifices (v. 4) and back into his high priestly garments (vv. 23–24; compare Ex. 28:1–43; for a visual depiction of the high priest's robes, see the *ESV Study Bible,* page 208). Discuss the significance of the high priest wearing plain linen robes for the sacrifices and changing into his glorious robes afterward. (Compare Isa. 61:3.)

Instructions for Regular Observance (16:29–34)

The last paragraph gives instruction for the regular observance of the Day of Atonement. It is here that the only instruction is given concerning the congregation's role in this festival. What does it mean for the people to "afflict" themselves in their regular observance of this festival (vv. 29, 31)?

Read through the following three sections on *Gospel Glimpses, Whole-Bible Connections,* and *Theological Soundings.* Then take time to consider the *Personal Implications* these sections may have for you.

Gospel Glimpses

FREEDOM FROM SIN. One of the distinctive features of the Day of Atonement is the use of two goats for the people's sin offering. Typical sin offerings used only one goat to remove the stain of sin from God's presence. But the second goat is added on this occasion to further display the removal of sin's power and presence from among the people. This is a precious hope shared by every believer in both Old and New Testaments. Scripture encourages us with the glorious hope that, one day, sin's power and temptation will be fully removed from our experience, never to be felt again. (See 1 Cor. 15:42; Heb. 12:23; 2 Pet. 3:13; 1 John 3:2–5; Rev. 6:11.)

GREAT HIGH PRIEST. Few rituals of the old covenant captured the humility and glory of the high priest's office as profoundly as the Day of Atonement. The simple linen garments the high priest wore in the Most Holy Place to atone for the people's sins were probably to demonstrate his humility as the congregation's sin bearer. The change into his glorious robes of beauty after the completion of the ritual suggests the honor God places upon him on account of his intercession for the people, and the delight with which the Father accepts his continual approaches thereafter with prayers on behalf of the people. The New Testament book of Hebrews tells us that the Old Testament high priest was a shadow of the Great High Priest, Jesus, who has entered into the heavenly Most Holy Place with the blood of our atonement and now stands in glory to intercede for us. (See Heb. 2:17–18; 4:14–16; 8:1–6; 9:6–14; 10:11–14.)

Whole-Bible Connections

MOST HOLY PLACE. In the ancient world, temples were designed as palaces for the gods. The tabernacle was likewise designed as a palace for the true God of Israel. But one difference was especially striking with respect to this divine "palace" compared to the temples of other nations. Other nations had an idol seated on a throne in their temple's inner sanctum, but the tabernacle had no image of God in its throne room. In fact, the tabernacle (and later the temple) did not even have a throne but only a footstool—the ark of the covenant—from God's throne (see Ps. 99:5). When other nations mocked Israel for having a temple without a "god" inside, Israel countered, "Why should the nations say, 'Where is their God?' Our God is in the heavens; he does all that he pleases. Their idols are silver and gold, the work of human hands" (Ps. 115:2–4). The design of the Most Holy Place was a reminder to Israel that this "divine palace" on earth was not the literal house of God, nor were its rituals the literal source of atonement. They were earthly shadows of the real atonement the true High Priest would present to God in the real temple—heaven itself (Ex. 25:40; Heb. 8:5; 9:24).

Theological Soundings

AN EXCLUSIVE GOSPEL. Leviticus 16 begins with a reminder (v. 1) of what happened to Nadab and Abihu when they attempted to approach God's presence by unauthorized means. The passage then states, "Tell Aaron . . . not to come at any time into the Holy Place inside the veil, before the mercy seat that is on the ark, so that he may not die. . . . But in this way Aaron shall come into the Holy Place" (vv. 2–3). Praise God, there is a sure and effective way to enter his presence and be accepted with life and heaven's blessings! But there is only one way. It is only through the sacrifice foreshadowed in the Levitical atonement rituals and accomplished by the Great High Priest, Jesus Christ (see John 14:6).

> **Personal Implications**

Take time to reflect on Leviticus 16:1–34 and its climactic lessons on atonement. Make notes below on personal implications of the (1) *Gospel Glimpses*, (2) *Whole-Bible Connections*, (3) *Theological Soundings*, and (4) this passage as a whole.

1. Gospel Glimpses

2. Whole-Bible Connections

3. Theological Soundings

4. Leviticus 16:1–34

As You Finish This Unit . . .

The complexities of the Levitical rites of atonement should fill our hearts with awe and gratitude for the great salvation accomplished for us by Jesus Christ. As you come to the end of this study of the Day of Atonement, let the insights you have gained stir praise and adoration in your heart. Spend time in prayer, speaking to the Lord about your response to his grace.

Definitions

[1] **Pentateuch** – The first five books of the Bible.

[2] **Intercession** – Appealing to one person on behalf of another. Often used with reference to prayer.

WEEK 8: HOLY AND UNHOLY MEATS

Leviticus 17:1–16

This passage begins the section of Leviticus that scholars call the Holiness Code (chs. 17–26). This name is used because of the repeated emphasis on being holy. Though scholars generally treat chapters 17–26 as the Holiness Code, Leviticus 20:22–27 seems like a conclusion to the purity and holiness law groupings. Therefore it is best to think of chapters 17–20 as holiness laws complementing the purity laws of chapters 11–15. Viewed this way, these groups of purity laws and holiness laws mirror each other, following the same basic outline:

	Purity Laws (Leviticus 11–15)	Holiness Laws (Leviticus 17–20)
Food Laws	11:1–47	17:1–16
Sexuality Laws (Part 1)	12:1–8	18:1–30
Main Body of Laws (purity laws on life overcoming death, and holiness laws on love overcoming sin)	13:1–14:57	19:1–37
Sexuality Laws (Part 2)	15:1–33	20:1–27

Leviticus 17 opens the holiness[1] section with laws on diet corresponding to the purity laws on diet in Leviticus 11. We previously learned that eating pork or touching a dead rodent made a person ritually unclean. We now learn that eating a sacrifice meal with "goat demons" or in communion with any false god is not just unclean but morally sinful (Lev. 17:7, 9). New Testament Christians rarely encounter pagan[2] sacrifice meals like those addressed in this chapter, but the imperatives we study here will help us think more carefully about the importance, "whether you eat or drink, or whatever you do," of doing "all [to] the glory of God" (1 Cor. 10:31).

The Big Picture

God's people are to enjoy worship meals only with him, abstain from communing or uniting with other gods, and eat all our food to God's glory.

Reflection and Discussion

Leviticus 17 opens with commands concerning the slaughter of livestock (vv. 1–9). These laws are followed by rules about consuming blood (vv. 10–12). The chapter ends with laws about the slaughter of hunted game (vv. 13–14) and the consumption of livestock that died accidentally (vv. 15–16). Read the entire chapter, then use the following questions to guide your reflection.

Domestic Livestock and Consuming Blood (17:1–12)

When Israelites hunted wild game like deer or gazelle, they were permitted to slaughter their kill for meat without sacrificing it. However, if Israelites wanted to slaughter domestic livestock like sheep or cattle, it had to be done by sacrifice. This restriction would change once Israel settled in the land, dwelling in cities far away from the sanctuary (see Deut. 12:20–22). However, prior to that time, all domestic livestock was to be slaughtered by sacrifice. With this background, read again the purpose statement for this law about domestic livestock (Lev. 17:5, 7) and discuss its significance.

Verse 4 makes the astonishing statement that shedding the blood of a sacrificial animal without bringing it to the altar was akin to bloodguilt (i.e., the shedding of human blood)! Why do you suppose the spilling of blood that could have been used for human atonement, without using it for that purpose, was treated like an attack on human blood (v. 11)?

Breaking purity laws required ritual washing. But the present laws introduce a new penalty: to be "cut off from the people" (vv. 4, 9, 10, 14). This probably means excommunication[3] from the tabernacle as one who has renounced the covenant.[4] Why would these violations of sacrifice laws be treated as evidence that an Old Testament Hebrew had denied faith in God's covenant? (Compare 1 Cor. 11:27–32.)

Wild Game and Livestock Killed by Accident (17:13–16)

Verses 13–14 raise the topic of hunted game. Consult the following passages and list the animals mentioned that the Israelites would hunt: Deuteronomy 12:15, 22; 1 Samuel 26:20; Amos 3:5.

When cattle died through natural causes or from a wild beast, a poor farmer may have wanted to salvage its meat. It was not considered a sin to do so, even though this animal was not slain by sacrifice. The farmer could eat the meat, but he would be ritually unclean. Review Leviticus 11:39–40; how do the purification rites in Leviticus 17:15–16 compare to that passage?

Read through the following three sections on *Gospel Glimpses*, *Whole-Bible Connections*, and *Theological Soundings*. Then take time to consider the *Personal Implications* these sections may have for you.

Gospel Glimpses

THE TRUE BLOOD OF ATONEMENT. The blood of animals was never to be treated as the actual source of life for the offerer (see Heb. 10:4). If animal sacrifices had been the actual source of forgiveness, Old Testament offerers likely would have been commanded to consume the animal's blood. As noted already, some ancient religions did command sacrificers to unite with an animal's life and imbibe its strength by consuming its blood. The prohibition against this practice in Israel was a profound rejection of any thought that animals could, in themselves, atone for human sin. In fact, Leviticus 17 says, "I will set my face against that person who eats blood and will cut him off from among his people" (v. 10). Rather than establishing the Hebrew worshiper within God's covenant, placing faith in the animal itself brought exclusion from God's people! Old Testament animal sacrifices were always intended to point to *the* Lamb of God who would come to take away the sins of the world (John 1:29; see Ps. 40:6–7; see also the discussion of "Lamb of God" on page 15, above). It was therefore not a contradiction of Old Testament law but a harmonious fulfillment of it when Jesus introduced the command to partake in his blood at the New Testament communion table. He is the One whose blood is the actual source of our atonement. The Levitical prohibition against blood consumption pointed to the true blood of atonement provided on the cross.

Whole-Bible Connections

CONSUMING BLOOD. In Acts 15, the apostles and elders met in Jerusalem to discuss whether Gentile Christians should be required to keep the Mosaic law. At that meeting the leaders of the New Testament church concluded that Gentile believers should not be expected to keep the Old Testament rituals, since the rituals were merely pointers to Christ. Many Jewish Christians at that time, however, still observed the Mosaic law (compare Acts 21:17–26), and continued to do so until God removed the temple (Acts 6:14; Heb. 8:13). For this reason, the Jerusalem Council required Gentile believers to observe certain limited strictures that would allow law-observant Jewish Christians to eat at the same table with them. Among those requirements was the command not to eat blood (Acts 15:20, 29). That requirement is rooted in the prohibition in Leviticus 17. Some Christians believe that this New Testament text means Christians must still abstain from blood. Others believe that all observance of the Mosaic rituals was to end with the destruction of the temple in AD 70 and that the restriction against blood in Acts 15 also expired at that time.

Theological Soundings

GUARDING THE TABLE. In 1 Corinthians 11:23–32, the apostle Paul gives instruction for the proper observance of the Lord's Table, drawing upon the truths found in Leviticus 17. In Leviticus 17, failing to guard the blood of sacrificial animals was likened to sin against human blood (Lev. 17:4). In the New Testament, failing to honor the communion elements is sin against the blood of Christ (1 Cor. 11:27).

HONORING GOD AT OUR TABLES. Leviticus 17 reports that many of the Israelites were sacrificing from their herds to "goat demons, after whom they whore" (v. 7). Believers today might not find the prospect of goat demons all that enticing, but the lesson in this text is more relevant than might first appear. Israel was attracted to goat demons because such worship allowed them to slaughter and eat their herds in their own fields (v. 5). Rather than going to the trouble to take livestock to the tabernacle as "sacrifices of peace offerings" (v. 5; see Lev. 7:12–15), it was considerably easier to slaughter them in rituals "in the open field," at home (17:5). The root sin exposed in this passage is one of failing to give God praise, giving glory to others instead. Modern believers won't likely turn to goat demons when they eat, but failing to give God thanks continues to be a common temptation faced by New Testament believers. Paul's instruction is relevant: "Whether you eat or drink, or whatever you do, do all to the glory of God" (1 Cor. 10:31; compare 1 Tim. 4:4–5).

Personal Implications

Review what you learned in this study of Leviticus 17:1–16, and make notes below on personal implications of the (1) *Gospel Glimpses*, (2) *Whole-Bible Connections*, (3) *Theological Soundings*, and (4) this passage as a whole.

1. Gospel Glimpses

2. Whole-Bible Connections

3. Theological Soundings

4. Leviticus 17:1–16

As You Finish This Unit . . .

Give thanks that the blood of Christ, the perfect Lamb of God, was given on the cross to "make atonement for your souls" (v. 11). We have the joy of confessing our union with him at every service of communion. Praise God for this gift now, and harbor the lessons of this passage in your heart for reflection the next time you participate in communion.

Definitions

[1] **Holiness** – A quality possessed by something or someone set apart for special use. When applied to God, it refers to his utter perfection and complete transcendence over creation. God's people are called to imitate his holiness (Lev. 19:2), which means being set apart from sin and reserved for his purposes.

[2] **Paganism** – Any belief system that does not acknowledge the God of the Bible as the one true God. Atheism, polytheism, pantheism, animism, and humanism, as well as numerous other religious systems, can all be classified as forms of paganism.

[3] **Excommunication** – In the NT, a form of church discipline that revoked a person's privileges as part of the community of believers. Typically imposed for unrepented sin or heresy, to preserve the community's purity and hopefully to bring the offender to repentance (Matt. 18:15–18; 1 Cor. 5; 2 Cor. 2:5–11; 1 Tim. 1:18–20).

[4] **Covenant** – A binding agreement between two parties, typically involving a formal statement of their relationship, a list of stipulations and obligations for both parties, a list of witnesses to the agreement, and a list of curses for unfaithfulness and blessings for faithfulness to the agreement. The Old Testament is more properly understood as the old covenant, meaning the agreement established between God and his people prior to the coming of Jesus Christ and the establishment of the new covenant (NT).

Week 9: Holy and Unholy Moral Conditions

Leviticus 18:1–20:27

The Place of the Passage

This section contains a general collection of laws about holiness (ch. 19), surrounded by commands about sexual purity (chs. 18 and 20). It follows the same pattern as that used for purity laws earlier in the book (see chart on page 55, above). Because of the strangeness of some laws in this section (e.g., 19:26–28) and the stunning variety of topics addressed, this portion of Leviticus can seem bewildering in many points. However, the overarching emphasis woven through the whole section is clear: "You shall be holy, for I the LORD your God am holy" (19:2).

The Big Picture

Because God atones for sin and dwells in the midst of his people, we are to anticipate victory over sin, separation from worldliness, and growth in godliness.

> ### Reflection and Discussion

As we have seen elsewhere in Leviticus, this passage is constructed as a chiasm. The following structure places emphasis on the center point (c), where we find the command Jesus quotes in his summation of the law: "You shall love your neighbor as yourself" (see Matt. 22:39).

a. Sexuality laws: marital integrity (18:1–30)

   b. Be holy—related to one another (19:1–18)

      c. "You shall love your neighbor as yourself" (19:18)

   b'. Be holy—separated from the Canaanites (19:19–37)

a'. Sexuality laws: community integrity (20:1–27)

The following reading selections are grouped topically based on the above outline. Read each selection as indicated, stopping after each to respond to the reflection guidance provided.

Sexuality Laws: Marital Integrity (18:1–30)

Leviticus 18 teaches sexual purity, beginning with the integrity of relationships within the extended family. Verses 6–18 define the extent of violations deemed incestuous. Two cases did not require mention (a daughter and a full sister) since they were obviously protected by the command not to violate "close relatives" (v. 6). The rest of the passage extends that standard to the whole family tree. Compare verses 6–18 with the following chart and discuss your observations.

Prohibited (Incestuous) Relations in Leviticus 18:1–18

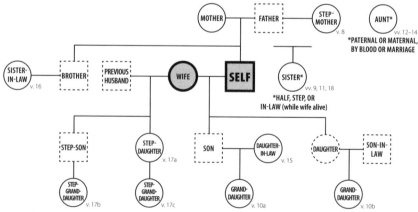

Verse references indicate persons mentioned in the passage with whom sexual relations would be incestuous and therefore are prohibited. The only legitimate sexual relationship in the entire family tree is that between the man and his wife. (Relatives with dotted outlines are shown for reference only.)

Verses 19–23 list sexual sins beyond the family circle: fornication (v. 19), adultery (v. 20), sodomy (v. 22), and bestiality (v. 23). What is the significance of the prohibition against offering children to Molech (v. 21) in the center of this grouping? (Note: v. 19 is probably not about the timing of a man's relations with his wife, a matter addressed in Lev. 15:24. This verse is likely about fornication with an unmarried woman, something typically pursued when the woman was least likely to conceive; compare Ezek. 18:6; 22:10.)

Sexuality Laws: Community Integrity (20:1–27)

This chapter returns to the themes of sexual integrity introduced in chapter 18. It is framed by prohibitions against child sacrifice (vv. 1–5) and consulting dead ancestors (vv. 6, 27). These practices were likely intended to secure blessings on the family line. What was the actual outcome of such practices (vv. 22–23)?

The fact that sexual laws (vv. 10–21) are grouped with laws about child sacrifices (vv. 1–5) and consulting dead ancestors (vv. 6, 27) or cursing living parents (v. 9) indicates that this text is not simply about sexual lust. These are laws about building a family heritage, and doing so in holiness (vv. 7–8, 22–26). Use the chart below to note ways in which these ancient challenges to a godly heritage are mirrored by moral confusion in our own day. How can Christians improve our testimony of God's holiness in the way we carry on a godly heritage?

	Violations	Notes
Fertility rites	(vv. 1–5) Child sacrifice	
Ancestor rites	(v. 6) Necromancy	
Call to holiness (vv. 7–8)		
Rebellion	(v. 9) Cursing parents	
Illicit sexual relations that violate another man's marriage	(v. 10) Violating a neighbor's wife	
	(v. 11) Violating a father's wife	
	(v. 12) Violating a son's wife	
Illicit sexual relations that violate the natural order	(v. 13) Violating another man	
	(v. 14) Violating a woman and her mother	
	(vv. 15–16) Violating an animal	
Illicit sexual relations	(v. 17) Violating an unmarried step-sister	
	(v. 18) Violating an unmarried single woman (see note on 18:19, above)	
	(v. 19) Violating an unmarried aunt	
Illicit sexual relations whose offspring would confuse family inheritances	(v. 20) Violating an uncle's wife	
	(v. 21) Violating a brother's wife	
Call to holiness (vv. 22–26)		
Ancestor rites	(v. 27) Necromancy	*(see v. 6, above)*

Be Holy, for I the LORD Am Holy (19:1–37)

Between the chapters on sexual holiness, Leviticus 19 presents an additional collection of wide-ranging laws on being holy as God is holy (v. 2). Look through the chapter for the repeated phrase "I am the LORD" or "I am the LORD your God." How many times do these phrases appear? _____

There are more than 30 commands in this chapter. The following chart shows how they are arranged into groups, with each group punctuated by the phrase, "I am the LORD (your God)." How does each group combine laws that reinforce one another? For example, in verses 5–10 a law about God's table is paired with a law about food for the poor. Joining these commands links a love for the Lord's table with a concern for the tables of the poor. If you are doing this study on your own, pick two or three of these groups of laws to ponder further and record your insights. If you are doing this study in a group, divide these sections among yourselves and then share your insights with one another.

Fostering a Holy Culture	Separating from Canaan's Unholy Culture
"You shall be holy, for I the LORD your God am holy." (v. 2)	*"You shall keep my statutes." (v. 19a)*
Revere parents. Keep the Sabbaths. *"I am the LORD your God." (v. 3)*	Do not confuse your produce. Do not confuse a vulnerable woman's status. Do not confuse the Lord's firstfruits and your fruits. *"I am the LORD your God." (vv. 19b–25)*

Fostering a Holy Culture	Separating from Canaan's Unholy Culture
Do not turn to idols (false gods). Do not make gods of metal (to represent the Lord). *"I am the LORD your God." (v. 4)*	Do not practice Canaanite ritual meals. Do not practice Canaanite divination. Do not practice Canaanite dedication rites. Do not practice Canaanite grieving rites. *"I am the LORD." (vv. 26–28)*
Do not profane holy food from the Lord's table. Do not fail to provide for the poor from your harvests. *"I am the LORD your God." (vv. 5–10)*	Do not adopt Canaanite cultic prostitution. Honor the Lord's worship times and place. *"I am the LORD." (vv. 29–30)*
Deal honestly with property. Deal honestly with people. Deal honestly with God. *"I am the LORD." (vv. 11–12)*	Do not consult mediums or necromancers. Do not seek them out. *"I am the LORD your God." (v. 31)*

Fostering a Holy Culture	Separating from Canaan's Unholy Culture
Do not take advantage of a vulnerable neighbor. Do not take advantage of a vulnerable worker. Do not take advantage of a physical vulnerability. *"I am the LORD." (vv. 13–14)*	Honor the elderly. Fear your God. *"I am the LORD." (v. 32)*
Do no injustice as a judge. Do no injustice as a witness. *"I am the LORD." (vv. 15–16)*	Do not take advantage of strangers. Show love to strangers as brothers. *"I am the LORD your God." (vv. 33–34)*
Do not let bitterness fester against a brother. Do not take revenge against a brother. *"You shall love your neighbor as yourself: I am the LORD." (vv. 17–18)*	Do not use unjust measurements. Use just measurements. *"I am the LORD your God who brought you out of the land of Egypt. . . . I am the LORD." (vv. 35–37)*

As the structural centerpiece of the holiness section (chs. 17–20), how does Leviticus 19:18 summarize the nature of holiness (compare Matt. 22:39; Rom. 13:9)?

Read through the following three sections on *Gospel Glimpses*, *Whole-Bible Connections*, and *Theological Soundings*. Then take time to consider the *Personal Implications* these sections may have for you.

Gospel Glimpses

RESTORED TO GOD'S IMAGE. Mankind was created to live in joyful communion and shared perfection with God—in other words, to live in *holiness*. But sin broke our relationship with God and deformed our reflection of his likeness (Rom. 3:10–19). On the one hand, Leviticus 19 convicts us of our sinful condition by its repeated emphasis on the command we cannot attain: "You shall be holy, for I the LORD your God am holy" (19:2). However, read in its full context—namely, as part of the laws on purity (chs. 11–15) and holiness (chs. 17–20) set in orbit around the Day of Atonement (ch. 16)—the same words also minister as words of promise to the atoned: "You shall be holy, for I the LORD your God am holy." This is the great hope that the apostle John echoes: "See what kind of love the Father has given to us, that we should be called children [i.e., image-bearers] of God; and so we are. . . . Beloved, we are God's children now, and . . . when he appears we shall be like him, because we shall see him as he is. And everyone who thus hopes in him purifies himself as he is pure" (1 John 3:1–3).

Whole-Bible Connections

SEXUAL PURITY. The standard of sexual purity throughout Scripture is tied to the vision set forth in Leviticus 18 and 20. For example, 2 Samuel 13:1–19 tells the tragic story of Amnon's violation of his half sister Tamar (Amnon's sister by the same father but different mother; compare Lev. 18:9). As Amnon was about to force Tamar, she pleaded, "No, my brother, do not violate me, for such a thing is not done in Israel" (2 Sam. 13:12). Her cry was rooted in the standards of sexual purity taught in Leviticus 18. Remarkably, the parameters established in Leviticus 18 also critique the marriages of some of the patriarchs,[1] like Abraham, who married his half sister (Gen. 20:12; compare Lev. 18:9), and Jacob, who took a "woman as a rival wife to her sister" (Lev. 18:18; see Gen. 29:21–30). None of the Bible's heroes, until Jesus, measure up to the holiness of perfect Godlikeness.

LOVING NEIGHBOR. The structure of Leviticus 19 suggests that the command to "Love your neighbor as yourself" is more than just another law on the list. In its position at the center of the list, it serves as the heart of what the chapter teaches about what it means to be holy. This significant role is further indicated by how the New Testament writers and other law experts of their day (Luke 10:25–28) regarded this verse as an important summary of the whole law (Matt. 5:43; 19:19; 22:39; Mark 12:31; Luke 10:27; Rom. 13:9; Gal. 5:14; James 2:8).

Theological Soundings

HOLINESS. Most people think the term *holiness* refers to a constraining, abstract ideal. But Leviticus 19 repeatedly emphasizes that holiness is not abstract but relational. Holiness is the very likeness of God, and human holiness can be attained only by relationship to the holy God. Furthermore, since God is supremely joyful in his holiness, we are led by a passage like Leviticus 19 to regard holiness as freeing rather than constraining. Holiness is a deliverance from the misery of worldly corruption and entrance into true, divine pleasure.

Personal Implications

Review what you learned in this study of Leviticus 18:1–20:27, and make notes below on personal implications of the (1) *Gospel Glimpses*, (2) *Whole-Bible Connections*, (3) *Theological Soundings*, and (4) this passage as a whole.

1. Gospel Glimpses

2. Whole-Bible Connections

3. Theological Soundings

4. Leviticus 18:1–20:27

As You Finish This Unit . . .

Leviticus 19 describes holiness in contrast with the kinds of sins and temptations Israel was to face in the land of Canaan. Think about the same high calling to Godlike holiness as it contrasts with our culture today. Humble your heart before God in a prayer of repentance, and let the promise of holiness through Christ's atonement also fill your prayer with praise.

Definition

[1] **Patriarch** – The earliest ancestors of Israel, primarily Abraham, Isaac, and Jacob.

WEEK 10: PERFECTION OF PRIESTS AND SACRIFICES

Leviticus 21:1–22:33

▲

The Place of the Passage

When the director of a play lines up actors, costumes, and props, every effort is made to ensure the arrangement will communicate the play's story. In a similar manner, the laws about the priesthood in this passage are carefully designed to make the tabernacle's message clear to worshiping Israelites. We have already studied an earlier passage about the appointment of a holy priesthood in the time of Aaron (chs. 8–10). In Leviticus 21–22, we revisit the topic of the priesthood, this time encountering laws that ensure the continuation in every generation of the message of hope for a perfect priesthood.

The Big Picture

Every generation of God's people must be taught the promise of a perfect priest who offers a perfect sacrifice for the congregation's atonement.

> ## Reflection and Discussion

This passage contains instruction in the following arrangement:

a. Laws on priestly perfection (21:1–24)

   b. Laws on priestly consumption of sacrificial foods (22:1–16)

a'. Laws on sacrifice perfection (22:17–33)

Read each of these passages in turn, pausing to complete the discussion guidance for each segment.

Priestly Perfection (21:1–24)

Did God care about a priest's physical blemishes more than his heart? Of course not (see 1 Sam. 16:7). But part of the picture of atonement put on display in the tabernacle was the physical wholeness of the priest (see Lev. 21:16–24). Why do you suppose that was the case?

Israel's priests were not allowed to grieve while on duty, even if a close family member died. They could weep at home, but why was it deemed inappropriate—from a symbolic perspective—for the ministers of atonement to weep while on duty?

The genealogies of the Bible are full of the same twists and turns as modern complicated families, with divorces, remarriages, multiple unions, single parents, and the like. What would it mean to Israel for the priestly genealogy to be carefully guarded and "uncomplicated" by these typical issues?

Priestly Consumption of Sacrifice Foods (22:1–16)

Chapter 22 has two parts: qualification of the priest to eat the sacrifices' remainders (vv. 1–9) and qualification for others to share in the sacrifices' leftovers at the priest's table (vv. 10–16). What are these two sets of regulations designed to teach (see vv. 9 and 16)?

Many ancient societies turned their sacrifices' leftovers into a business by selling them in the market for the profit of the priests. (See the note on 1 Cor. 8:1–11:1 in the *ESV Study Bible*, page 2202.) How would the restrictions in this passage have guarded against that practice in Israel?

Sacrifice Perfection (22:17–33)

Compare the 12 points of sacrificial perfection (22:22–24) with the 12 points of priestly perfection (21:18–20). What similarities and differences do you observe? (Note, the final blemish on each list refers to sexual wholeness, and the four blemishes in 22:24 refer to methods for gelding livestock.)

_____

_____

_____

_____

_____

_____

A freewill offering is one brought spontaneously. A vow offering is one brought in fulfillment of a prior promise. What does the more lenient allowance for a freewill offering in verse 23 imply?

_____

_____

_____

_____

_____

_____

Read Isaiah 53:1–5 and 1 Peter 1:13–20. Based on those two texts, what did the Old Testament prophet and the New Testament apostle learn from these Levitical laws of sacrifice?

_____

_____

_____

_____

_____

_____

Read through the following three sections on *Gospel Glimpses*, *Whole-Bible Connections*, and *Theological Soundings*. Then take time to consider the *Personal Implications* these sections may have for you.

Gospel Glimpses

PERFECT SACRIFICE. Old Testament believers, most of whom were farmers, would have appreciated the value of a perfect specimen of livestock as described in Leviticus 22:21–25. Such perfection, combined with its proven viability after surviving at minimum its first full week of life (vv. 26–27), indicates that the animal in view had no reason in itself to die. It would have been a choice specimen of great value, full of life and reason to live. Only such a sacrifice, with no reason in itself to die, could serve as the substitute for the sins of the offerer. The requirement of a perfect sacrifice taught the Old Testament worshiper to trust in God's promise of a sinless Mediator[1] to complete the required atonement (Isa. 53:1–5; 1 Pet. 1:13–20).

PERFECT SACRIFICER. During the intertestamental[2] period, some Jews thought God would send a single messiah[3] to fulfill all the roles required of him. Others thought God would send more than one messiah, each to fulfill the different tasks required. Ultimately, Jesus undertook all the duties of our atonement himself. Remarkably, Jesus became our perfect Prophet and also the perfect Word proclaimed; he became our perfect King and also our perfect Servant; he undertook the duties of the perfect Priest promised in Leviticus 21, as well as the perfect Sacrifice promised in Leviticus 22. The work of Christ is mind-boggling in its scope and elegance. Everything it took an elaborate tabernacle system and fully staffed priesthood, palace, and prophetic circle to accomplish was finally realized in a single person: Jesus Christ.

Whole-Bible Connections

SLAVERY. The Old Testament view on slaves has been a source of controversy throughout history, and the present passage is one of a handful in Old Testament law that speaks about slaves. Some scholars believe the Mosaic law contained contradictory standards on slavery. Verses like Leviticus 22:11 (and 25:39–46) have often been understood to permit slave ownership in Old Testament Israel, while passages like Exodus 21:16 strictly forbade slavery and slave ownership (compare Deut. 23:15–16). The apparent contradiction disappears, however, when we recognize that the kind of slavery approved in Old Testament Israel was debt slavery—bondage to work off debts—and not chattel slavery (that is, owning humans like animals). Furthermore, those attached to the household to work off debts were to be treated like members of the family. For example, Leviticus 22:11 says that debt slaves in priestly families could eat sacrifice leftovers with the priest's family, while hired servants could not. The only distinction between a debt slave and a member of the family was that the debt slave worked on the family estate for a limited period of years, did not receive pay for that work, and did not have an inheritance in the household. Regardless of the size of the debt, a maximum of seven years' labor was permitted (Deut. 15:12–18; see the Week 11 "Reflection and Discussion" notes on Lev. 25:1–55). Although biblical laws like Leviticus 22:11 have often been interpreted to support chattel slavery, a careful study of the relevant passages does not support that conclusion. Although Israel had a system of debt slavery so that households that defaulted on loans could work off their debts, Old Testament law introduced provisions to ensure that such labor would not deteriorate into chattel slavery—like the slavery Israel had experienced while in Egypt and was never to impose on anyone else (see Lev. 19:33–34; compare Job 31:13–15).

Theological Soundings

JOYFUL SERVICE. Undoubtedly, it would have been difficult for priests to leave the burial of loved ones to other family members. The restrictions in Leviticus 21:1–4, 10–12 do not prohibit a priest from grieving the loss of extended family, but the priest must leave the ritually defiling process of burial to others. These restrictions were put in place not to make things difficult for the priests but rather to uphold the portrait of a joyful, life-ministering priesthood (compare 2 Sam. 19:1–8). The beautiful attire of the high priest (Ex. 28:1–43), his melodic movements in performing his sanctuary duties (Ex. 28:33–35), and his abstention from all marks and practices of grieving (Lev. 21:1–5, 10–12) portray a vibrant and joyful priesthood. Contrary to the common stereotype that priests were dour figures, the priesthood Christ undertakes is one filled with joy: "For the joy that was set before him [he] endured the cross" (Heb. 12:2).

PERFECTION. The nation of Israel was organized in "social rings," with those suffering from the most deathlike physical disease (leprosy) residing on the outskirts of the camp, those experiencing the day-by-day imperfections of life dwelling in the camp itself, those unmarred by impurity or physical defect being able to serve in the tabernacle courts, and the individual high priest alone entering the holy place as one in perfect physical form. All of these—reaching all the way to those dwelling on the outskirts of the camp—were part of Israel and members of the community of the atonement. The increasing perfection visibly portrayed by this system as one moved closer to God's presence was not a message of exclusion for the afflicted, but a portrait of promise regarding what all God's people could anticipate one day in his presence (see Ps. 16:11). The 12-fold lists of physical perfections ascribed to the priest and to the sacrifice in Leviticus 21–22 communicate this idea of complete perfection.

Personal Implications

As you reflect on what you have learned in this study of Leviticus 21:1–22:33, note below any personal implications about the (1) *Gospel Glimpses*, (2) *Whole-Bible Connections*, (3) *Theological Soundings*, and (4) this passage as a whole.

1. Gospel Glimpses

2. Whole-Bible Connections

3. Theological Soundings

4. Leviticus 21:1–22:33

> ## As You Finish This Unit . . .

Read 2 Corinthians 5:21 and meditate on the moral perfections of Christ as your True Sacrifice and Sacrificer. Spend time in praise and prayer for his satisfaction of heaven's justice on your behalf, that you might have hope for complete moral, physical, and spiritual wholeness in the Father's presence.

Definitions

[1] **Mediator** – One who intercedes between parties to resolve a conflict or achieve a goal. Jesus is the Mediator between God and rebellious humanity (1 Tim. 2:5; compare Heb. 9:15; 12:24).

[2] **Intertestamental** – Pertaining to the time between the end of OT history and the beginning of NT history. Roughly 430–5 BC.

[3] **Messiah** – Transliteration of a Hebrew word meaning "anointed one," the equivalent of the Greek word *Christ*. Originally applied to anyone specially designated for a particular role, such as king or priest. Jesus himself affirmed that he was the Messiah sent from God (Matt. 16:16–17).

Week 11: Observing the Sacrifice Festivals

Leviticus 23:1–25:55

The Place of the Passage

Electricity, food preservation technologies, and climate control have enabled modern societies to operate almost unrestrained by the natural seasons. But in the ancient world, far more than in our own day, the seasons set the cadence for life and labor.

Calendars were used in biblical times to track the changing seasons of the year and manage one's farm in cooperation with seasonal cycles. Because each nation sought blessing on their labors from their god(s), worship festivals were attached to key points in their agricultural calendars. Each nation's worship calendar revealed what they believed about the relationship between their yearly labors and the heavens. In Israel, the agricultural calendar was attached to festivals commemorating the events of the exodus[1] from Egypt, because Israel understood their labors as service to the true God of redemption.[2]

Mirroring the section explaining the sacrifices and sacrifice meals (Leviticus 1–7), the present passage (Leviticus 23–25) describes the calendar of Israel's sacrifice festivals.

The Big Picture

God gives his people a cadence of worship to keep their lives and labors anchored in the blessings of redemption.

Reflection and Discussion

There are four calendars combined into this section of Leviticus:

a. Israel's weekly calendar (23:1–3)

b. Israel's annual calendar (23:4–44)

c. Addenda to the weekly and annual calendars (24:1–23)

d. Israel's generational calendar (25:1–55)

Read the sections about each of these calendars, stopping after each reading to reflect using the guidance questions below.

Weekly Calendar (23:1–3)

Before discussing the seasonal holy days of the Israelite calendar, the Lord first provides guidance for the weekly holy day—the Sabbath. What instructions were given for how this weekly Sabbath was to be observed (v. 3)?

Annual Calendar (23:4–44)

Israel had seven annual festivals, four in the spring (vv. 4–22) and three in the autumn (vv. 23–44). Compare the following chart to the passage and note any observations. (Note: The Hebrew year began in the spring, around the time we call March or April today.)

SPRING FESTIVALS	Date	Agricultural Significance	Exodus Story Connection	Notes
Passover (23:4–5)	1st month, 14th day	First full moon of the year; time of spring equinox	Passover in Egypt (Ex. 12:1–51)	
Unleavened Bread (vv. 6–8)	7 days beginning on 1st month, 15th day	Time of spring equinox	Exodus from Egypt (Ex. 13:3–10)	

SPRING FESTIVALS	Date	Agricultural Significance	Exodus Story Connection	Notes
Firstfruits (vv. 9–14)	"day after the Sabbath"—first Sabbath of harvest season	First sheaf (time of barley harvest)		
Weeks (vv. 15–22)	7 weeks after Firstfruits	"New grain" offering (time of wheat harvest)	Arrival at Mount Sinai (Ex. 19:1)	
AUTUMN FESTIVALS	Date	Agricultural Significance	Exodus Story Connection	Notes
Trumpets (vv. 23–25)	7th month, 1st day	Time of autumn equinox		
Day of Atonement (vv. 26–32)	7th month, 10th day	Time of autumn equinox		
Booths (vv. 33–44)	7 days beginning on 7th month, 15th day	"When you have gathered in the produce of the land" (final harvest, including grapes, sheep shearing, etc.)	Journey through the wilderness to the Promised Land (Lev. 23:42–43)	

Which of the annual festivals were marked by joy? Which were times of mourning and repentance?

The last festival of the year was the Feast of Booths. This feast was to remind every generation that "I made the people of Israel dwell in booths when I brought them out of the land of Egypt" (v. 43). In other words, God took care of the people on their journey. Why do you suppose the festival year ended with a reminder of God's care on the people's journey to the land, rather than ending with a celebration of arrival in the land?

Calendar Addenda (24:1–23)

The regular calendars of Israel (weekly and annual) close with three addenda. The first two relate to scheduled chores of the priests tending to the lampstand (vv. 1–4) and the table of showbread (vv. 5–9). The lamp represented God's life-giving presence with the people. The 12 loaves represented the people's presence before God. What would be the significance of including these maintenance routines in this calendar?

The final addendum to Israel's annual calendar is the story of a blasphemer's[3] punishment (vv. 10–23). The focus of the text is on the blasphemer's Egyptian heritage. We have already learned that sojourners are to be treated with the same love as neighbors (19:33–34). This passage teaches that sojourners, while not compelled to participate in Israel's worship, were required to respect it. Why do you suppose such a sober lesson would be added to the end of Israel's annual worship calendar?

Generational Calendars (25:1–55)

Many scholars think the Sabbath Year, like the annual festivals, was tied to agricultural reality: the need for a regular time of letting the land remain fallow to avoid depleting soil nutrients. Fields were not to be farmed and harvested during the Sabbath Year (vv. 4–5); nevertheless, subsistence food production was permitted (v. 6). What does this provision suggest about God's care for the land?

The final layer of Israel's calendar was the Year of Jubilee, observed every seventh Sabbath Year. The Jubilee was a once-a-generation economic reset. Even if one generation fell so deeply into debt that the next was raised in debt slavery and the family property was lost, the Jubilee Year ensured the emerging generation would receive it back. What do you think was the significance of this proclamation of liberty taking place on the Day of Atonement during the Jubilee Year (v. 9)?

Non-Hebrew debt slaves had to continue their service obligation into the next generation—at least until their debt was satisfied (vv. 44–46). What evangelistic impact might this have had on indebted foreigners in Israel?

Read through the following three sections on *Gospel Glimpses*, *Whole-Bible Connections*, and *Theological Soundings*. Then take time to consider the *Personal Implications* these sections may have for you.

Gospel Glimpses

SABBATH. The Levitical calendar is designed around the Sabbath principle and its promise of rest (Gen. 2:1–2; compare Ex. 20:8–11; Neh. 9:14). The weekly Sabbath[4] was the foundational holy day of the whole calendar (Lev. 23:3). From there, the Sabbath principle was extrapolated throughout the calendar by repeated patterns of seven. There were seven festivals in Israel's yearly calendar, all within the first seven months of the year. There were seven weeks between the festivals of Firstfruits and Weeks. The festivals of

Unleavened Bread and Booths were each seven days in length. The Sabbath Year occurred every seven years, and Jubilee occurred after seven sevens of years. Through these and other patterns of sevens, the entire calendar is rooted in the Sabbath principle, spreading the promise of divine rest through the entire system.

Whole-Bible Connections

NATURE'S WITNESS. In the New Testament, the apostle Paul wrote that God's "invisible attributes, namely his eternal power and divine nature, have been clearly perceived, ever since the creation of the world, in the things that have been made" (Rom. 1:20; compare Acts 17:26). The calendar of Old Testament Israel drew numerous connections between the nature of God and the demonstrations of his goodness in the seasons. Paul's proclamation might have had in view those "clearly perceived" demonstrations of God's goodness in the changing seasons of the year, as captured in the calendar of Israel.

ISRAEL'S FESTIVALS. In both the Old and the New Testaments, numerous events take place against the backdrop of the festivals of Israel's calendar. For example, the Gospel of John describes many events in the life of Jesus during the Old Testament festivals of Leviticus (see John 2:23; 5:1; 6:4, 22; 7:2, 23, 37–39; 10:22; 13:1; 19:14, 31, 42; 20:1).

Theological Soundings

SUNDAY WORSHIP. The practice of gathering together in local communities for worship every week is rooted in the Sabbath principle stated in Leviticus 23:3. In Old Testament times, weekly assemblies were held on the seventh day of each week. Most Christians have historically viewed the resurrection of Jesus from the dead on the first day of the week as indicating a change in the day for worship to the first day of the week. This understanding is based on Jesus' command, after his resurrection, for the disciples to regather to meet with him in worship on the first day of the week (Luke 24:13–49), a pattern repeated by the New Testament church (compare Acts 20:7; 1 Cor. 16:2).

Personal Implications

What have been the most significant lessons you have learned from your study of Leviticus 23:1–25:55? Note below any personal implications you have gleaned from the (1) *Gospel Glimpses*, (2) *Whole-Bible Connections*, (3) *Theological Soundings*, and (4) this passage as a whole.

1. Gospel Glimpses

2. Whole-Bible Connections

3. Theological Soundings

4. Leviticus 23:1–25:55

> ## As You Finish This Unit . . .

Meditate on the ways the atonement of Christ has fulfilled various promises set forth in the Old Testament festivals, from becoming our Passover Lamb to his ascending before us into the true "Promised Land." Praise God for accomplishing all that he promised, and pray for grace to fix your heart on heaven as you look forward to the eternal Sabbath.

Definitions

[1] **The exodus** – The departure of the people of Israel from Egypt and their journey to Mount Sinai under Moses' leadership (Exodus 1–19; Numbers 33). The exodus demonstrated God's power and providence for his people, who had been enslaved by the Egyptians. The annual festival of Passover commemorates God's final plague upon the Egyptians, resulting in the people's release from Egypt.

[2] **Redemption** – In the context of the Bible, the act of buying back someone who had become enslaved or something that had been lost to someone else. Through his death and resurrection, Jesus purchased redemption for all believers (Col. 1:13–14).

[3] **Blasphemy** – Any speech, writing, or action that slanders God. In the OT, the penalty for blasphemy was death (Lev. 24:16); in the NT, Jesus states that the one who blasphemes against the Holy Spirit will not be forgiven (Luke 12:10).

[4] **Sabbath** – Saturday, the seventh day of the week, the Jewish day of worship and rest (Gen. 2:2–3; Ex. 31:13–17). Christians meet for worship on Sunday, the day of Christ's resurrection (Acts 20:7), and regard Sunday, rather than Saturday, as their weekly day of rest. And yet, believers look forward to an eternal Sabbath rest (Heb. 4:1–13).

WEEK 12: BLESSINGS AND DISCIPLINE

Leviticus 26:1–27:34

▲

The Place of the Passage

Ancient treaties and covenants were typically sealed with concluding blessings and curses. The book of Leviticus has such a conclusion in chapter 26, although the "curses" in that chapter are not what one might normally expect. Furthermore, a list of congregational responses—vows, dedications, devotions, and tithes—in chapter 27 invites the readers to hear the "blessings and curses" and respond in renewed devotion and worship.

The Big Picture

God is eager to draw wandering prodigals to himself, and he goes to great lengths with great patience to do so.

Reflection and Discussion

The closing chapters of Leviticus include a "blessings and discipline" section (ch. 26) and a "response" section (ch. 27). Read these chapters one at a time, stopping to study them with the guidance questions below.

Blessings and Discipline (26:1–46)

Read Genesis 3:8–9 and Revelation 21:3–4. Compare those passages to the promise in Leviticus 26:11–12. Why do you suppose the Bible frequently describes the believer's ultimate hope in this manner? (For extra reading, compare also Ex. 6:7; 29:45; Jer. 7:23; 11:4; 24:7; 30:22; 31:33; Ezek. 11:20; 14:11; 36:28; 37:27; 2 Cor. 6:16. A word search through the Bible will produce even more passages that repeat this same promise.)

The purpose of God's blessing is to draw his people closer to himself (Lev. 26:11–13). Normally, we would expect those blessings to be countered with curses of separation. However, the curses section of Leviticus 26 contains not curses but discipline (compare Heb. 12:5–11). What is the purpose of the discipline God promises to those who wander after other gods (see Lev. 26:18, 21, 23, 27, 40–45)?

This chapter contains 11 verses about blessings upon the faithful, and 32 about discipline. What does this proportion suggest about the nature of God's people? What does it tell us about the nature of God's love?

Renewal and Rededication (27:1–34)

Chapter 27 seems an odd addendum after the blessings and disciplines in chapter 26, until we recognize the purposes of these vows (vv. 1–13), dedications (vv. 14–27), devoted things (vv. 28–29), and tithes (vv. 30–34). Each of these special offerings was in response to God's blessings or discipline. This passage gave Israelites guidance, after discerning their location on the list of blessings or discipline in the previous chapter, to respond. What types of gifts were Israelites likely to present (either literally or through a financial valuation) in these various offerings?

The valuation of persons (vv. 1–8) is not based on the actual worth of a life (compare Ps. 49:7–8). These are valuations based on a person's estimated earning potential. As a vow offering of thanks, an Israelite might present his or another family member's labor as a debt slave of God's house until the next Sabbath-year release. What would your estimated labor valuation be on this list? _____

Gifts of labor ("vows"; Lev. 27:1–13) and property ("dedications"; vv. 14–27) were typically restored to the original owner at the next Sabbath-year release. "Devoted things," however, were surrendered permanently to God (vv. 21, 28–29). Something was devoted usually out of repentance or to purge idolatry from the community. A gold idol, for example, or wealth gained sinfully would be devoted to God in repentance (compare Josh. 6:18–19). Sorcerers and priests of false gods who led the community astray would also have been subject to such purging if they did not repent (v. 29). Read Leviticus 20:22–27 (compare

Deut. 18:9–14) and discuss why you think Leviticus 27:28–29 introduces such a stern warning concerning sorcerers and pagan priests.

Vows, dedications, and devoted things were brought as gifts of renewal. "Tithes" (27:30–33) were regular expressions of ongoing faithfulness. What form of giving do you believe to be appropriate today for expressing a Christian's dedication and thanksgiving to God?

Read the last verse of Leviticus (27:34) and the first verse of Numbers (1:1). What change takes place in the location of God's communication with his people because of the gift of atonement put into operation in the book of Leviticus?

As you reflect on this study of Leviticus, read Romans 3:21 and discuss how the laws of Leviticus, though unable (and never intended) to accomplish eternal righteousness[1] in themselves, bore witness to the righteousness accomplished by Christ. How have you grown to understand the work of Christ and to love him more through this study?

Read through the following three sections on *Gospel Glimpses*, *Whole-Bible Connections*, and *Theological Soundings*. Then take time to consider the *Personal Implications* these sections may have for you.

▶ Gospel Glimpses

"I WILL BE YOUR GOD." The 17th-century Puritan preacher Thomas Goodwin once said, "If I were to go to heaven, and find that Christ was not there, I would leave immediately, for heaven would be hell to me without Christ." Goodwin understood that the joy of our salvation is not the promise of a certain place but restoration to a relationship with our glorious Creator through the self-sacrifice for us of our glorious Redeemer. The heart of the gospel as expressed throughout the Scriptures and in the closing of Leviticus is the promise of communion with God: "I will make my dwelling among you.... And I will walk among you and will be your God, and you shall be my people" (Lev. 26:11–12; compare Ex. 6:7; 29:45; Jer. 7:23; 11:4; 24:7; 30:22; 31:33; Ezek. 11:20; 14:11; 36:28; 37:27; 2 Cor. 6:16; Rev. 21:3–4).

NO MORE OFFENSE. The Hebrew word translated "abhor" in Leviticus 26 (vv. 11, 30, 43, 44) expresses the sense of revulsion one feels from something that makes the stomach churn. Leviticus uses this word to describe the kind of offense that human sin is in the eyes of God (v. 30). We fail to appreciate the true nature of our sin until we come to recognize the deep, stomach-churning offense it is before God. However, the blessing and cursing sections of Leviticus 26 both culminate in the twice-repeated promise that God's soul "shall not abhor you" any longer (vv. 11, 44). The marvel of the atonement is that human sin is so perfectly resolved that God's people are clean and genuinely pleasing in his sight. Because of the atonement taught in Leviticus and accomplished by Christ, God's soul takes true delight in his people.

▶ Whole-Bible Connections

ISRAEL'S DISCIPLINE. The punishments outlined in Leviticus 26:14–45 correspond to the kinds of discipline experienced by Israel in the rest of Old Testament history: fear and privation from marauding enemies (Lev. 26:14–17; Judg. 6:2–6), famines (Lev. 26:18–20; Ruth 1:1; 1 Kings 17:1–7), wild animals (Lev. 26:21–22; 2 Kings 17:21–26; Ezek. 5:17), invasions and war (Lev. 26:23–26; 2 Kings 17:1–18), and exile[2] with all its horrors (Lev. 26:27–45; 2 Chron. 36:15–21). The fifth series of punishments—exile and all its horrors—so closely parallels the Babylonian exile account of 2 Chronicles 36:15–21 that it is likely that the author of Chronicles intended to show the fulfillment of God's warning from Leviticus in how he reported that event. But by doing so, he also shows that the Babylonian exile was not divine abandonment but discipline for the purpose of restoration (see 2 Chron. 36:22–23).

Theological Soundings

COVENANT. The word *covenant* appears once in the series of promised blessings (Lev. 26:9) and seven times in the series of disciplines (vv. 15, 25, 42, 44–45). When the Lord pours out his blessings on his people, he does so to "confirm my covenant" with each generation of the faithful (v. 9). Conversely, when God disciplines the unfaithful, he nevertheless refuses to abandon them utterly, because of his "covenant with Jacob . . . with Isaac, and . . . with Abraham" and "with [Israel's] forefathers, whom I brought out of the land of Egypt" (v. 42, 45). Remarkably, God's blessings and disciplines are both shown to bring the same result: a faithful people belonging to the Lord (vv. 11–13, 44–46). This stubborn grace of God, who refuses to abandon his people, is rooted in his relation to them through covenant.

OFFERINGS. Leviticus contains many regulations for the sacrifices brought to the tabernacle. Chapter 27 introduces a series of offerings brought in various forms of dedication that supported the house of God but were not presented as sacrifices at the altar. Many scholars think this chapter was added at the end of the book to show the importance of financially supporting the work of God's house. The pattern of both free-will offerings and regular tithes that continues to be observed in many churches finds its basis, in part, in the instructions at the end of Leviticus.

Personal Implications

In the spaces below, write down the personal implications you have drawn from the (1) *Gospel Glimpses*, (2) *Whole-Bible Connections*, (3) *Theological Soundings*, and (4) from Leviticus 26:1–27:34 as a whole.

1. Gospel Glimpses

2. Whole-Bible Connections

3. Theological Soundings

4. Leviticus 26:1–27:34

> ## As You Finish This Unit . . .

As you complete this study of Leviticus, read the account of the Last Supper and the crucifixion of Christ (Luke 22:7–23; 23:1–46) with newfound insight from Leviticus. Then pray to thank God for the gift of atonement, responding with your own repentance and renewed devotion in service and faith.

Definitions

[1] **Righteousness** – The quality of being morally right and without sin. One of God's distinctive attributes. God imputes righteousness to (justifies) those who trust in Jesus Christ.

[2] **The exile** – Several relocations of large groups of Israelites/Jews have occurred throughout history, but "the exile" typically refers to the Babylonian exile, that is, Nebuchadnezzar's relocation of residents of the southern kingdom of Judah to Babylon in 586 BC. (Residents of the northern kingdom of Israel had been resettled by Assyria in 722 BC.) After Babylon came under Persian rule, several waves of Jewish exiles returned and repopulated Judah.

Experience the *Grace* of God in the *Word* of God, Book by Book

KNOWING THE BIBLE STUDY GUIDE SERIES

· · · · · · · · · ·CURRENT VOLUMES· · · · · · · · ·

Genesis	Proverbs	Mark	Galatians
Exodus	Ecclesiastes	Luke	Ephesians
Leviticus	Isaiah	John	Philippians
Joshua	Jeremiah	Acts	Colossians and Philemon
Ruth and Esther	Daniel	Romans	Hebrews
Ezra and Nehemiah	Hosea	1 Corinthians	James
Psalms	Matthew	2 Corinthians	Revelation

crossway.org